IT'S NEVER TOO LATE

IT'S NEVER TOO LATE

Getting Older, Wiser, and Worry-Free
in Our Golden Years

Scott Page

New York

IT'S NEVER TOO LATE

Getting Older, Wiser, and Worry-Free in Our Golden Years

Published in New York, New York, by Morgan James Publishing. Morgan James and The Entrepreneurial Publisher are trademarks of Morgan James, LLC.
www.MorganJamesPublishing.com

The Morgan James Speakers Group can bring authors to your live event. For more information or to book an event visit The Morgan James Speakers Group at www.TheMorganJamesSpeakersGroup.com.

A **free** eBook edition is available
with the purchase of this print book.

CLEARLY PRINT YOUR NAME ABOVE IN UPPER CASE

Instructions to claim your free eBook edition:
1. Download the BitLit app for Android or iOS
2. Write your name in **UPPER CASE** on the line
3. Use the BitLit app to submit a photo
4. Download your eBook to any device

ISBN 978-1-63047-623-6 paperback
ISBN 978-1-63047-624-3 eBook
Library of Congress Control Number:
2015905333

Interior Design by:
Bonnie Bushman
The Whole Caboodle Graphic Design

In an effort to support local communities and raise awareness and funds, Morgan James Publishing donates a percentage of all book sales for the life of each book to Habitat for Humanity Peninsula and Greater Williamsburg

Get involved today, visit
www.MorganJamesBuilds.com

Habitat
for Humanity®
Peninsula and
Greater Williamsburg
Building Partner

Dedication

This book is dedicated to my dear friend Steve Terrell. Without your unwavering commitment, brilliant ideas, and masterful execution, this book would never have been possible. Throughout our lives, you have always seen my true potential.

Thank you, thank you, thank you.

XOXO

Table of Contents

Acknowledgements

I am grateful to so many individuals for the gifts of inspiration, love, and support throughout my life and more specifically during the writing of this book. My special thanks go to:

Betty White for her friendship and priceless life lessons for living life to its fullest.

Joel Brokaw for his expertise in getting my words down on paper with ease and enjoyment.

Raelene Mercer of Sublime Miami for her wonderful graphic design.

Wil Gilmore for his humorous illustrations that more than hit the target.

My family, last but not least, for their unwavering love and support and for setting me forth on such an interesting life.

Introduction

For many years, I have had the privilege of working to help thousands of people prepare for their older years and secure a better future for themselves and their families. So many of these people who have reached out to me have found themselves in troubled waters financially as they've approached retirement age. Their experiences, which have caused me to feel both frustration and hope, have been distilled into this book. The frustration has come from seeing over and over again the train wreck of highly preventable problems. The hope stems from seeing the dramatic turnaround when some of the solutions in this book are put into action.

Many of the steps I outline in the following chapters speak to basic common sense. They may include advice you have heard before, but that is where the similarity ends. What separates my plan from the others will hopefully be easy to notice not long after you start reading. As noted above, much of what I offer draws on the lessons I've learned firsthand helping people find solutions in times of diminishing choices. But in truth, I don't have to look much further than the drama in my own immediate family to illustrate how most of us have already shot ourselves in the foot before ever taking a first step.

What we will remedy together in the pages of this book are some of the complex and once formidable factors that got us mired in this big mess to begin with and have collectively locked us in a downward spiral. You will discover in *It's Never Too Late: Getting Older, Wiser, and Worry-Free in Our Golden Years* that more solutions are available than most people realize. Once you take action, you'll be relieved to see how long-term patterns of self-defeating thinking and behaviors start to lessen their hold.

The success I've experienced in dealing with the challenges in my life is based on the simple axiom of having a plan and putting it in motion. For that reason, this book is very pragmatic. It excludes intellectual concepts that make sense on paper but go in one ear and out the other. Instead, the first part of the book is holistic in nature and will help you quickly move beyond the fears related to growing old and approaching death that are at the core of the whole problem. Once lifted, you will be empowered to address the many choices that are presented in the second part of the book. Most importantly, you will be able to secure the finances to take care of your core essentials like keeping a roof over your head and putting food on the table.

It's Never Too Late is written for people who want the straight facts and don't want to be soft-sold on the one hand or scared to death on the other. Personal responsibility and dedication are crucial ingredients you need to bring to this process. Be mindful through it all how distraction, procrastination, wishful thinking, and denial lurk to knock you off course. What I want to help you avoid is human nature's tendency to wait until the last minute, when a situation has deteriorated into a full-blown disaster, when the whole mess could have been prevented if addressed earlier. Far too often, these disasters happen to good people who trusted what they were told and thought they were doing the right thing. Again, the information I present will help you recognize potential trouble spots and equip you to make sound decisions on the things that matter most to the quality of your life as you get older.

One important note: you do not need to follow each and every suggestion in this book in order to experience a successful outcome. Some of the items on the menu may not apply to your individual situation. Others may be too far beyond your comfort zone. But just the acts of contemplation and dialogue can have a positive impact. Even if you turn only one of my suggestions into action, it can have a transformative effect and make the time we spend together a valuable experience for us both. You may also be able to use some of the information to help others going through similar challenges. After all, there are few more gratifying and empowering human experiences than the simple act of sharing and helping one another.

Part 1

THE GROUNDWORK

"I can't retire."

"I have no idea how I'm going to support myself and my family in the coming years."

"I don't know where to start, and it's probably too late to do anything about it anyway."

For many individuals, confusion, fear, and an overwhelming sense of powerlessness accompany the prospect of growing old in America. According to a recent opinion survey conducted by Harris Polls, over 70% of people in their fifties do not think they have saved enough to live a comfortable lifestyle after they stop working. A full third of the middle-aged within the middle class are depressed about their prospects. And most shockingly, 22% of middle-income adults polled responded that they would rather die early than run out of money in old age.

It wasn't until the last 15 or 20 years that it became routine to hear about older people struggling to make ends meet. The cost of living was significantly lower a few decades ago than it is now, but there are a lot of additional factors at work, too. The good news is that we have more power to address this situation than we think.

Upon closer examination, it's not terribly surprising to find so many older Americans in this predicament. Like the old children's tale "The Emperor's New Clothes," what's surprising is that so few experts have focused on what seems pretty obvious—our basic unwillingness to deal constructively with the realities involved in approaching retirement and the end of life. Regrettably, there are a host of issues we would rather not think about, let alone creatively and proactively plan for.

At the root of the problem and at the heart of the solution are deeply entrenched attitudes that keep many of us paralyzed in a state of denial, avoidance, or wishful thinking. Unfortunately, this is the equivalent of hearing a tsunami warning and refusing to move to higher ground. It's as if we believe we are invincible heroes with superpowers that will allow us to swim or surf our way out of our predicament. Yet as many are now experiencing, if we fail to take action, the things we fear most will inevitably come crashing down upon us and sweep us away.

Personal finance experts publish tons of books with the best-intentioned advice on this subject. Unfortunately, most of it falls on deaf ears because of our preexisting condition: the unrealistic if not delusional ways in which we see ourselves. In fact, many of these books are never read cover to cover because of our multiple layers of resistance. I hope your experience here will be a notable exception.

One false belief that baby boomers hold to a degree unlike previous generations is that they are somehow going to live—and work—forever. They carry on without a plan for the future like they have an exemption from the process of diminishing health, dying, and eventual death. "That only happens to others," they think.

Many also hold tight to a vision of "retirement" that is a relic of the twentieth century, when people wore out in their sixties and expected to live out their remaining few years feeding pigeons in the park. That old model (feel free to substitute idling in a rocking chair on the porch) is no longer realistic for most people. Besides, in the big picture, it's neither fulfilling nor healthy. The fact is, many of us are living longer than ever and have seen our nest eggs (if we were lucky enough to have saved one) fall victim to stock market volatility. We've also seen our pension plans evaporate and the value of our real estate crash.

Nonetheless, it's not too late to stop clinging to beliefs that are better suited for fairy tales and to deal with the realities of a rapidly changing world. What I hope to do in Part 1 is open the door to some simple but profound ways we can each be better guardians of our destinies.

Freeing ourselves from our fears about growing old and embracing the abundant choices before us may at first seem overwhelming, but hopefully, after reading this book, you will be surprised at just how easy it can be. You

Chapter 1

Reality Check

As so often happens, my own wake-up call on the subject of living well in retirement was a personal one. I remember how devastating it was to witness the hope and faith my parents once had for their golden years shatter and dissolve into disappointment, confusion, mistrust, and fear. It became apparent to me through witnessing their journey that living well in old age hinges on self-sufficiency and independence. If we don't have financial flexibility, we can't make our own decisions, and if we can't make our own decisions, we really can't take care of ourselves.

My father, Tom Page, is a proud yet humble man in his late seventies, a retired steelworker who, like your typical baby boomer, believes in the virtue of hard work. At a party to celebrate his retirement from Bethlehem Steel after forty years with the company, I met many of his co-workers for the first time. It is no exaggeration to say that over the years, my father spent more time with these people than he did with my mother Grace, my late older brother Tracy, my younger sister Becky, and me. He was so dedicated to his job as a master welder that he once joked he wished he had a cot at work so he could stay and nap between shifts.

At his retirement party, his friends told many stories I had never heard, all on the themes of how much he loved his family and how no job was too hard for him. They described how he would crawl into the tightest spaces and climb up the tallest scaffolds to get the job done, feats no one else would dare attempt. It was all living proof of the degree to which he had given his life to the company, and in more ways than one. His lungs were destroyed by asbestos, his joints shackled with severe pain, and his body weakened to the point that any further corrective surgery was deemed too high a risk.

His retirement party was bittersweet. I was so upset when I heard his employers had not planned anything in his honor that I scrambled to rent the Baltimore VFW hall and send out invitations. I wanted to present him with the traditional gold watch, so I gave him my 1963 vintage Rolex (made the year I was born) that I'd bought when I first started earning decent money, engraving it to commemorate the occasion. I salvaged my father's retirement, but the indignity of his treatment by the company he had faithfully served for so many years was trivial compared to what followed.

Just like the old Baltimore Colts notoriously pulled up stakes and left town in the cover of night, America's second largest steel manufacturer also suddenly vanished from the landscape. First went the health care coverage my dad so deserved and needed when the company folded in bankruptcy in 2001 and was sold off. Then the pension plan he had paid into over the years, which had been matched by the company, vaporized. Those were the funds that would have allowed him and my mother to maintain the financial quality of life they had worked so hard to create.

It was all such heartbreak, but it also opened my eyes. You see, what happened to my parents and millions like them could have been prevented with a little more practical foresight and planning. Nonetheless, my parents have never regarded themselves as victims. They are too proud. They are the kind of people who always try to make do, never wanting to ask others for help. But the reality of their situation, had it been left unchecked, is sobering. Without skillful crisis intervention, I am almost certain they would not be alive today because of all the stress. While no one could have foreseen the company's closure or the demise of the pension plan, such events clarify how essential it is to diversify to protect against such events.

The undeniable truth is that there are good reasons to worry about how we are going to survive in our golden years due to our avoidance of the issues and our paralyzing inaction. In addition to the Harris Poll I cited earlier, the media continuously stokes our fears and anxieties with nightmarish facts about how ill-prepared most of us are. Another such report I recently read estimated the mean retirement savings per American household at a paltry $3,000!

In fact, the whole notion of "retirement" is on the endangered species list. This lifestyle enjoyed by our grandparents in the twentieth century and some of our fathers and mothers in decades past is increasingly rare. On a positive note, it does afford an opportunity for innovation.

A new vision is desperately needed, because today's older and aging Americans live under economic and social conditions far different from their parents and grandparents and thus have different needs and desires. First and foremost, people are living longer and have the tools to live healthier, more active, lives. They no longer want to sit at home collecting what once were adequate pensions. At the same time, the nuclear family is no longer the primary defining social structure (as witnessed by the high rates of divorce, remarriage, and the gender equality movement). In turn, this change requires us to challenge many of our outdated assumptions, but none of this is possible until we first turn the mirror on ourselves and take a much-needed personal inventory to get a true handle on our resources and capabilities.

Make no mistake—there were economic challenges back in the days of my grandparents, too. My grandfather used to own gumball machines, and as a child, I would sometimes go around with him to some really seedy places to take care of them. I would help him collect pennies and nickels out of the machines before restocking them with a variety of little trinkets that we placed inside small plastic bubbles. It was a simple business model. As my grandfather explained, "If you can buy it for a nickel and sell it for a dime, you're making money."

I asked him one day, "Paw Paw, you're retired, so why are you out here on Saturday and Sunday mornings doing this?"

He answered, "I've got to take care of myself." This work ethic, conditioned into me by both my grandfather and my father, is that we have to do whatever we can to take care of our families and ourselves. Some of that same spirit of personal responsibility, work ethic, and good old-fashioned common sense will come in handy for you as you roll up your sleeves to tackle whatever mess you're facing.

While I'm on this topic, I want to give a short public service announcement to point out the fact that many older people discount or underestimate the value of their wisdom. I'm not sure if my grandfather was aware of the lifelong influence his "buy it for a nickel, sell it for a dime" statement had on me. Sometimes the examples we set and the advice we give may not feel well received but may stick more than we realize. We shouldn't be discouraged when we don't receive immediate positive affirmation. It goes along with that generosity of spirit idea of giving without any expectation of getting anything back.

Happily, the book you have in your hands right now offers a workable plan for how to live out your life with greater peace of mind and security regardless of your current age and station in life. As long as you are well enough to get out of bed in the morning, you are fully capable of taking more positive control of your destiny. Like going to the gym to lose weight and improve your health, it will require some work, but the extraordinary difference it can make is unmistakable, both in immediate results and in long-term returns, and it all starts with a reality check.

Chapter 2

Breaking through the Wall of Resistance

I saw a commercial on television recently for a major investment brokerage firm that posed the questions "What does retirement mean for you?" and "What do you want to do in your retirement?"

Reflecting modern attitudes, the spectrum of responses ranged from having more time to travel and see the grandchildren to starting a new business to having the resources to get out and fully enjoy life. The image the ad put forward was positive and empowering—retirement is about living.

Toward that end, many seniors who have the ways and means are being pro-active about making positive changes and are putting themselves in situations that allow their wisdom base and life experiences to become valuable assets to others. One good example is how college towns like Austin, Texas, have become new retirement hotspots for seniors who thrive off of the energy of young people.

You may be asking, "What do all those vibrant, affluent people in the commercial have to do with the bulk of us who are unhealthy or struggling to make ends meet?"

I know it might sound cliché, but as long as you are alive, there is hope. You may not be able to pull up stakes and move to Austin, fly first class to Hawaii, or help pay for your grandchild's college education, but now is the time to look with appreciation at what you do have. Too many of us make ourselves sad and crazy about the things we desire but have not been able to acquire. Consider the fact that growing old and gray and going to bingo on Wednesday night is a privilege that is denied to many. It's time to smell the roses, even if all you have is a single rose. "I've got a great dog and a good roof over my head" is an example of one such positive affirmation you can build upon.

As mentioned earlier, perhaps the single most formidable barrier that puts effective retirement planning into critical condition involves that most irrational of beliefs that we're going to live forever. It's the same syndrome that plagues Baby Boomers who believe they can work indefinitely. Despite the deaths of family pets, grandparents, and others near to us, we carry on for most of our lives like we're indestructible until we are shocked back into reality by some alarming event. Then, after a brief sobering interlude, most of us simply return to our cherished illusions. This attitude, cloaked in our fundamental fear of losing our independence, has to be overcome if we want to make progress.

A frantic phone call from my mother a short while back shows how this illusion holds on tight with a tenacious grip.

"Your father is up on the roof!"

My mother was absolutely hysterical.

"What the hell is he doing up there?" I asked.

"There's a shingle loose, and he climbed up to fix it! What am I going to do?"

"Go out there and tell him to get down. Tell him I want to talk to him."

While I waited on the phone, my mother pleaded with my dad. In the background, I could faintly make out his stubborn voice insisting that he wouldn't come down until he'd "fixed the damned shingle."

I had been so concerned about my dad's bad hips, his open-heart surgery, and his asbestos poisoning, not to mention my mother's bad knees, that I'd moved my parents to a house where they no longer had to climb up and down stairs. We'd also had a number of memorable discussions about what my dad could and couldn't safely do at age 75, but after all, this was a man his co-workers had described as having no fear of heights. So, not surprisingly, he was up on the roof.

I didn't want my mother screaming at my dad to get down, so I told her, "Just get out there and watch him. Get ready to call 911. As soon as he gets off the roof, have him call me."

On the slippery slope down from the roof, my dad lost his footing and fell. The only thing that stood between him and a date with mortality was a single nail that caught him by the pants and halted his descent to the pavement below.

I could tell by his attitude on the phone a few moments after his near-death experience that he thought of this as just another day at the office, all in line with the experiences of a steelworker back in a time of lax occupational safety regulations.

"Dad, why did you get up on that roof?" I asked him.

"Well, one of the shingles blew off."

"Why didn't you call me? I'd have arranged to have somebody come fix it."

"I'm not calling you every time I need something. I live in this house. I'm the man. I should be able to take care of it. If I can't take care of this house, I have no business living here."

"Dad, I understand that, but you're putting yourself at risk by climbing up on the roof."

"Next time, I'll tie a rope around my waist and attach it to the chimney just in case."

Sarcasm aside, my dad never ended up fixing the shingle. He'd gone up on the roof to figure out what was going on and was coming down to get the right tool.

"Next time, I'll tie a rope around my waist and attach it to the chimney just in case."

Whether he'd admit it or not, he relented after our call, and we ended up having a professional come out and take care of the problem.

My father's pride and stubbornness are among many of the entrenched attitudes and behavioral programming that this book hopes to remedy. After all, there are some very real and pragmatic causes of fear, anxiety, anger, and hopelessness that can make it hard to listen to reason and take concrete action to put ourselves on a more positive track.

Perhaps the most crushing disappointment for many of us is the fact that the nest eggs we once counted on for support in our old age have either collapsed or are very slowly getting off the ground as a result of the economic downturn in recent years. Middle-class Americans counted on good returns on their most important investment— home ownership—until the mortgage crisis of 2008 burst the housing bubble. Since that time, declining property values have been devastating (unless properties were bought at low prices decades ago). Many seniors affected by this have scant hope that the lost value can be recouped in their lifetimes.

As happened to my parents, the economic downturn also saw millions lose their pension plans. Meanwhile, no one has found a politically acceptable answer to our nation's troubling long-term sustainability questions about Social Security and Medicare. It doesn't help that the media and advertising worlds are sending mixed messages about what matters most for our retirement and healthcare, confusing us and adding fuel to our growing distrust and angst.

As I tell those who come to me for professional advice, "We're all going to get old and die, and we need to plan for it." I say this not to jolt them but simply to be forthright because most people, when left to their own devices, choose the easier path of living a fantasy, regardless of whether times are good or bad. If my message is to be heard, some immense psychological and emotional barriers must be dismantled.

In addition, good planning in these changing times involves contingencies for big *and* small surprises. If we don't accept certain truths about the inescapable process of aging and death, we simply won't be able to put the important information in this book to good use. At the same time, accepting these truths does not mean they are imminent. In fact, planning for them can actually eliminate stress and help us savor longer, happier lives.

One of the most joyful aspects of my work is spending time with life-embracing elders such as the actress Betty White, who recognize that knowledge is power and who never stop learning. Now in her early nineties, Betty still chases life. She works. She uses her mind and body. She's out in the world sharing her wisdom and talents. She's hardly sitting around waiting to die. On the contrary, she believes, as I firmly do, in the four "P" words—*planning*, remaining *positive*, always being *proactive*, and remaining open to your own outstanding *potential*.

If you are ready to break through the wall of resistance around planning for your retirement, I have a simple and highly effective exercise that can act to jumpstart you. You might even laugh at the idea because it's so simple, but I guarantee it will get you off the dime and in motion.

What I'm asking you to do is to take out a pen and pad of paper and start listing any and all objects of value in your possession, whether they are material objects or things on paper like an insurance policy or an IRA. Then divide this list into the following categories:

1. Valuable objects you want to keep
2. Valuable objects you want to give away (or leave in your will to a loved one)
3. Valuable objects you don't need and could potentially sell

If you've been hoarding things your whole life, getting rid of them can be difficult, and that's why these categories can be helpful. There's that old Pontiac out in the garage collecting dust—maybe you'd be better off selling it or donating it to charity for a tax write-off. That silver collection from your grandmother up in the attic—you never use it, and it's such an unnecessary pain to polish. The family jewelry and watches sitting in a drawer, untouched for years—maybe you should figure out what to do with them instead of setting up your heirs for a knock-down, drag-out fight or, worse yet, having a probate judge make the decision. Wouldn't it just be easier to sell the jewelry on eBay or leave it to someone in a will? Loved ones brawling at a funeral over a ring on a finger happens more often than you might think and can easily be avoided.

List other assets on paper such as insurance policies, IRA and 401(k) accounts, Social Security payments, and anything that produces money. This is vital, because having only a vague idea of your true worth might leave you shooting from the hip and quite vulnerable when it comes time to make important decisions impacting your quality of life.

While accounting for your valuables, why not clean house and de-clutter and dispatch all the unnecessary things that are taking up valuable space? This is no different than when your computer is running slowly and you install a software program to clean up all the useless data you've accumulated. Your mind is like that hard drive that runs so much more smoothly once its bandwidth is freed up. Freeing up your bandwidth is reenergizing and refocusing, and it allows you to take better control of your destiny.

Getting your house in order can be liberating on a deeper level than you might realize, but I'm fully aware that most of us would rather climb up on the roof to fix a loose shingle than sit down and start this process. Going through old boxes in the closet, cellar, or attic can dredge up a lot of memories, some good and some bad, but hopefully therapeutic all the same.

Ultimately, by taking these steps, you've begun the process of freeing yourself from a lot of unnecessary fear and stress. When you open up to new opportunities, you realize how much easier it was than you ever expected to break through the fears and anxieties that once had such a stranglehold on you.

Chapter 3

Life Expectancy Planning

There was something peculiar on one of my IRA account statements recently. It nicely broke down what my monthly retirement income would be if I continued to make contributions to the fund at the same level. These calculations took into account my date of birth and the assumption that I would begin to claim my benefits at age 67, my full retirement age for Social Security. But what caught my eye was this statement: "We have calculated the monthly income in today's dollars you can reasonably expect your account to generate until age 84."

Translated more bluntly, I was being told, "We expect you to die at age 84. We predict that you will be okay until then."

Reading in-between the lines.

Any financial services company dealing with seniors is already running its own internal life expectancy calculations, but ask any employee, "How do you talk to your clients about mortality?" and you will get the same answer.

"We don't," as one reverse mortgage company executive told me. "We never tell the client, 'We expect you to live for five more years.'"

There is even a term for this called "moral hazard." This is that ethically shaky ground that tries to avoid any hint that the financial services company might cherish the thought of its elder client's demise so that it can take final ownership of the house or seize whatever asset has been promised.

I realize there's something big brotherish about the fact that both the government (the Social Security Administration) and the aforementioned private financial services companies are running these algorithms on us. In response, we may want to take the advice of the cartoon character Felix the Cat: "If you can't beat them, join them." Information is power, so why not take advantage of these same projections to make sound choices when it comes to important decisions about your future?

To determine when a client should take Social Security and for greater clarity on some of the other big decisions impacting quality of life in our golden years, I use a technology at my office that fills in an indispensable piece of the retirement planning puzzle. This tool, the life expectancy calculator, may also prod us to make changes that can help us live healthier and longer by giving us a probable estimate or a best educated guess of our life expectancy.

Life expectancy calculators merge personal data such as medical and family health history and lifestyle habits with statistics from the Centers for Disease Control and actuarial research from the insurance industry. Insurance companies and financial entities that lend or have long-term commitments with older adults use this data for many purposes, including setting loan amounts, terms, and interest rates and for overall planning and risk management.

Without factoring in probable life expectancy to your plans, you are essentially shooting in the dark. Consider what a difference it can make to know the statistical likelihood of living to age 86 versus age 72 when deciding whether to take Social Security sooner or later.

You might be asking yourself, "Do I really want to know an estimate of when I am predicted to die?"

If your answer is "No," you are among the majority of people who, like my mother, are happy keeping things just the way they are. Such individuals believe that if they don't think about it, talk about it, or plan for it, they can somehow avoid death. Regardless of whether or not you choose to do this calculation, the hardcore truth is that we all have an expiration date on our mortality. Likewise, we have three choices on how to handle that reality—we can deny it, we can ignore it, or we can plan for it.

Finding out your life expectancy estimate and conducting the kind of thorough retirement planning I strongly urge you to do would probably not be such a front-burner topic were it not for the fact that we're living much longer than we did a generation or two ago.

I also believe that the many benefits involved in confronting your life expectancy far outweigh the discomfort. Choose to view this data as a reference point, a challenge that you can both meet and exceed by making sound choices about the things that are truly in your power. In fact, all the financial decisions you make should use the minimum age of this estimate so that your planning will always involve adding an extra contingency percentage to cover the possibility of a longer lifespan.

At the same time, don't get overly attached or emotionally worked up over the findings. None of this is guaranteed. You may exceed the crunched numbers on that computer printout or you may not. Remember that supposedly healthy, "never been sick a day in my life" people drop dead all the time, and accidents and unforeseen circumstances can strike any of us today or tomorrow. That said, I know from personal experience that engaging in this process is easier said than done.

"When are we going to have our family conference?" I recently asked my mother on the phone. I wanted to share the findings I'd run on each of us.

"Oh, I'll have to check and see," she replied, which is code for "Avoid, avoid, avoid."

My motivation in running this information on my family was two-fold. First, I thought it was time to get serious and pull my head out of the sand. I knew that my mother's obesity and the stress management issues compounding my father's other health problems were life threatening. If they saw how taking better control of these problems could mean living an additional three, five, eight, or maybe even 10 extra good years, perhaps they would make those changes, be a better support to each other, and be less co-dependent.

The other good reason for going through all of this is one that all members of "the sandwich generation" will appreciate: I am the sole financial provider for my parents, but I'm also at an age at which I need to aggressively plan for my own retirement. I don't want to sound like the Grim Reaper, but having this data about them and myself means I'm on much firmer footing when making important decisions and setting priorities. I want the peace of mind that comes with knowing I'll have the wherewithal to meet my responsibilities in the long haul.

If you're open to exploring this process, I'd like to take you through a couple of examples of what a life expectancy projection looks like. The two case studies mapped out below may give you a foreshadowing of your own situation, but don't rely on them. Keep in mind that the complex math and data merge isn't something you want to tackle on your own with just a pencil, paper, and a pocket calculator. There are so many variables depending on your age, gender, and other factors that it would be an exercise in confusion, frustration, and futility. Instead, go to one of the online services recommended on my web resources page (www.ScottPage.com) to quickly and effectively have the higher math done for you.

Assuming you are an adult with average health, the first step in this introductory exercise is to look at the table below and find the baseline figure for the average life expectancy. "Average health" is somewhat subjective, of course, and varies depending on age and gender, so separate tables for male and female are used.

The number in the left hand column is your age as of your last birthday. The number in the right hand column indicates the number of years the statistical research predicts you are likely to live beyond your current age. The technology uses this "healthy, average" baseline as a starting point. Time is subtracted in statistical increments if you happen to smoke, are obese, have diabetes, drink alcohol excessively, abuse drugs, or suffer from a number of other conditions that are known to shorten lifespan (this includes heart disease, hypertension, Alzheimer's/dementia, and high cholesterol). Not exercising, failing to have regular medical check-ups, or having a genetic propensity for cancer or heart disease reduces the estimated number of years you will live to be. Note that likely terminal diseases such as late stage cancer are not considered here.

Average Life Expectancies for U.S. Residents		
Age at Last Birthday	Male Life Expectancy (in years)	Female Life Expectancy (in years)
35	44.4	46.7
36	43.5	45.8
37	42.5	44.9
38	41.6	43.9
39	40.7	43.0
40	39.8	42.3
41	38.9	41.2
42	38.0	40.3
43	37.1	39.4
44	36.2	38.5
45	35.3	37.6
46	34.5	36.7
47	33.6	35.9
48	32.8	35.0
49	31.9	34.2
50	31.1	33.3
51	30.2	32.5
52	29.4	31.7
53	28.6	30.8

Age at Last Birthday	Male Life Expectancy (in years)	Female Life Expectancy (in years)
54	27.8	30.0
55	26.9	29.2
56	26.1	28.4
57	25.3	27.6
58	24.6	26.9
59	23.8	26.1
60	23.0	25.3
61	22.2	24.6
62	21.5	23.8
63	20.7	23.0
64	19.9	22.2
65	19.2	21.5
66	18.4	20.7
67	17.7	19.9
68	17.0	19.2
69	16.3	18.3
70	15.5	17.6
71	14.8	16.8
72	14.2	16.1

Age at Last Birthday	Male Life Expectancy (in years)	Female Life Expectancy (in years)
73	13.5	15.4
74	12.8	14.7
75	12.2	14.0
76	11.6	13.3
77	10.9	12.7
78	10.3	12.0
79	9.8	11.3
80	9.2	10.7
81	8.5	10.0
82	7.9	9.3
83	7.3	8.7
84	6.6	7.9
85	6.0	7.3
86	5.5	6.8
87	5.0	6.3
88	4.6	5.8
89	4.3	5.5
90	4.0	5.2
91	3.2	4.3

Age at Last Birthday	Male Life Expectancy (in years)	Female Life Expectancy (in years)
92	2.7	3.6
93	2.4	3.3
94	2.2	3.1
95	2.0	2.8
96	1.9	2.6
97	1.7	2.3
98	1.6	2.1
99	1.5	2.0
100	1.4	1.9

On the other hand, factors such as maintaining a healthy weight, exercising, and getting health checks regularly plus enjoying a stable family life, living a stress-reduced lifestyle, and having a family history of longevity can add years to this baseline projection.

The following conditions are known to significantly shorten or lengthen life expectancy. Again, note that likely terminal conditions such as late-stage cancer are not considered and that these are average life expectancies. Actual lifespans will vary, so you should make financial decisions that account for the possibility of living well beyond your average life expectancy.

Common Conditions That Shorten Life Expectancy	Common Conditions That Lengthen Life Expectancy
Smoking	Familial longevity
Diabetes	Regular exercise
Obesity	Healthy weight maintenance
Excessive alcohol consumption	Regular doctor visits for colonoscopies, mammograms, etc.
Drug addiction	Regular mental stimulation
Hypertension	Stable family life
High cholesterol	Medical directive compliance
Lack of medical care	Healthy diet
Failure to follow medical directives	Stress-resistant personalities (Type B)
Sedentary lifestyle	
Genetic propensity for heart disease or cancer	
Depression	
Poor diet	
Sexual promiscuity	
Dementia/Alzheimer's	
Osteoporosis	
Stress-sensitive personalities (Type A)	

To give you a better sense of how these calculations are made, let's look at two case studies that break the process down unit by unit. In the following examples, you will see how the estimate ticks up or down based on each finding. The first case study shows a 70-year-old woman who is making many of the right choices to extend her life expectancy. The second case study demonstrates the potential outcome for a lesser compliant 65-year-old male.

Case Study One: 70-Year-Old Female		
Personal Description	**Life Expectancy (LE) in Years**	**Effect on LE**
70-year-old woman	17.6	Starting point from chart
Non-smoker	17.6	Non-smoking status is assumed in chart (No change in LE)
Responsible alcohol consumption	17.6	Responsible alcohol use is assumed in chart (No change in LE)
High blood pressure controlled by Rx	17.4	Hypertension shortens LE but effect is lessened by Rx control
High cholesterol controlled by Rx	17.2	High cholesterol shortens LE but effect is lessened by Rx control
Father died of heart attack at 75 years old	16.9	Shows a genetic propensity to heart disease and shortens LE
Mother lived to 92 years old	17.2	Parental longevity extends LE
Swims or gardens most days	17.8	Regular exercise extends LE

Personal Description	Life Expectancy (LE) in Years	Effect on LE
Healthy weight and diet	18.5	Healthy weight and diet extend LE
Regular colonoscopies and mammograms	19.1	Preventative medical care extends LE
Works part-time/active social life	19.7	Regular mental stimulation extends LE
Handles stress well	20.3	Effective stress management extends LE
RESULT:	**Mean LE of 20.3 years**	

Case Study Two: 65-Year-Old Male		
Personal Description	**Life Expectancy (LE) in Years**	**Effect on LE**
65-year-old male	19.2	Starting point from chart
Smoker	14.4	Smoking drastically reduces life expectancy
Responsible alcohol consumption	14.4	Responsible alcohol use is assumed in chart (No change in LE)
High blood pressure—noncompliant with Rx/poorly controlled	13.4	Uncontrolled hypertension shortens LE
Type A personality—often anxious/stressed	12.9	Poor stress management shortens LE
Fast-food-centered diet	12.2	Poor diet shortens LE
Father lived to 89 years old	12.4	Parental longevity extends LE
RESULT:	**Mean LE of 12.4 years**	

As you can see, a 70-year-old woman who makes responsible health and lifestyle choices has a significantly longer life expectancy than a 65-year-old male who makes more dubious choices.

The economic peace of mind this book strives to help you achieve is another factor that can effectively extend your life expectancy. Not having the kind of money worries plaguing many older Americans who have not planned well can keep you healthier simply by removing a major source of stress. It is fascinating how this so-called "wealth effect" is a significant factor in longevity up to age 80, after which genetics and lifestyle take over and play a far greater role.

Having a positive outlook, a good spiritual life (covered in the next chapter), and a firm sense of purpose can also increase your chances of winning the bet against these statistical models. If you possess these qualities, be sure to account for that extra longevity in your retirement plans!

Chapter 4

Getting Your
Spiritual Act Together

Warning: the whole topic of spirituality can be a minefield, so please hang in there with me and keep an open mind. This is not a chapter about religion or religious beliefs. It is not going to challenge whatever faith or belief system you have. But there would be a big hole in this book if I didn't bring this topic up because having your spiritual act together is a huge difference maker—it's the great intangible that is more powerful to your health and longevity than any of the factors tracked on the aforementioned life expectancy charts.

Science cannot explain why spirituality is so important. It's not something we can see or touch. But as I learned as a young man, it seems to be a common essence no matter where we turn or who we are in the wonderfully diverse human landscape.

While in boot camp in the Air Force back in the early 1980s, I overheard someone say that if you could sing, you could join the choir in an air-conditioned church on Sundays for a series of back-to-back services. The religious aspect of going to church didn't appeal to me. Since I loved to sing, my thinking went more like this: "Here's a way to get out of the heat and escape running drills for six hours every Sunday."

Growing up, my family wasn't churchgoing. Activities like being baptized, reading the Bible, and going to Sunday school were things other kids did. Thus, while I was lured to church by the air conditioning, what I got was exposure to the diverse faiths of my fellow recruits, a virtual Religion 101 crash course. The unexpected bonus I received was a great overview of the common spiritual ground shared by all faiths.

Although they each had varying names and archetypes to describe the divine, each faith seemed to be in unanimous agreement regarding the existence of a greater power. I also noticed something else that was extremely beneficial: regardless of whether we were praying to Jesus, Allah, Buddha, or the universe, something profound and expansive was happening. I saw firsthand that the simple act of having faith in a higher power we can neither see nor touch opens us up to new possibilities.

Before I go further, please let me repeat that this is not a pitch about religion. You do not have to believe in a god or any celestial being to tap into a mindset that helps develop your higher potential. Instead, I simply ask you to examine how often the big obstacle standing between you and a decent quality of life is often solely in your own mind and what you are consequently doing to yourself.

That common thread I just mentioned centers around two key elements, hope and faith. With hope and faith, we are grounded and centered. Without them, we don't have anything. To repeat, you don't need to become religious if you aren't already, but you do need to have faith in yourself, in the people with whom you associate, and in the way you live your life. Without hope, which is the opposite of despair, you remain a magnet for problems and adversity. You simply cannot move forward if you don't have hope and faith. If you have lost these and all you are left with is misery and despair, and if staying there is the decision you choose to make, your potential for manifesting growth is close to zero.

The antidote for this is the fact that you do have the power within (barring serious neurological impairment and mental illness) to make changes; you can learn how to replace despair and darkness with hope and light. It's not like you flick a switch and everything immediately becomes all right. You cannot go into a laboratory and create hope and faith. There is no pill to swallow that will fill the void. Instead, it's a life-long unfolding that grows inside you and renews itself with each passing day.

Transformation begins once you are truly willing to embrace this dimension. Some people come to greater spiritual awareness by enduring tragedy, facing adversity, or hitting rock bottom. However, just knowing there is room for improvement in this part of our lives can also get the ball rolling.

It sounds simple, but it's easier said than done. Human beings are highly resistant to change. Some people remain in a spiritual quagmire because they are content with not knowing a better outcome is available. They prefer to ignore reality and sit with their heads buried in the sand. Venturing out of their uncomfortable comfort zones is scary, like jumping off a diving board without checking first to see if there's water in the pool.

Personally, I don't believe this is a healthy or optimal way to live. I believe it means we have given up, and I don't think we can ever give up. If everyone decided to give up, human life as we know it would end. That's why hope and faith are so critical.

One important caveat is that we cannot move through life on blind faith, either. We cannot close our eyes and have faith that if we walk into the middle of the street, a truck won't hit us. There are critical limits to what I am saying, and I don't want the message to be blown out of proportion or taken out of context. The point is, our first essential step is to get in touch with our mortality. We have to take stock of what we have, be grateful for the things around us, and embrace a plan to improve.

Without a generous dose of hope and faith, I am certain I would hardly have accomplished anything of merit in my career as an entrepreneur. An entrepreneur is someone who is taught to believe in what they are doing and to follow their gut. A person like me does not come out of a business school like Harvard or Wharton, where graduates are formally trained to know the four corners in which they operate. If the Excel spreadsheet says "No," they don't proceed. Had I approached a professor at any reputable school with my business plan outlining an idea that would involve the multi-billion-dollar life settlement industry, he or she would probably have given me an "F." I can hear their voices of condemnation now: "Talking to people about selling their life insurance policies? Are you mad? That's not what life insurance is for!"

What hope and faith give is a sense of being at peace with ourselves. Being at peace also comes from planning and from fully understanding the options that are available before we rush to judgment. That old adage "Don't judge a book by its cover" is a simple statement packing a powerful truth. Many times, we have to peel back the skin of the onion to discover what is actually inside.

To repeat for emphasis, developing and nurturing our spiritual selves is not always all butterflies and roses or for the faint of heart. Sometimes we have to go inside the dark places where our secrets and worst fears hide. That's one reason spiritual happiness is so elusive. Turning from

Chapter 5

"Change Your Focus,
Change Your Future"

O ne of the most common ways we sabotage ourselves and limit or even destroy our potential is by giving negativity permission to live rent free in our lives. Negativity is so debilitating that it can feel like a genuine affliction, as if our imbalanced brain chemistry feeds on being in a perpetual downer state.

I have struggled with this myself. For example, I often wonder how a very dear lifelong friend and I can manage to go from zero to hate in a flash. When I replay various scenes in my head, I realize that the only thing I can change is how I choose to react when I perceive something to be negative. I know that changing my knee-jerk ways means taking real responsibility for what I think, say, and do. Otherwise, it's too easy to sit back and point the finger at how so-and-so is the cause of why I'm so miserable and why such-and-so has taken place.

Once we recognize the triggers, the things that spur our negativity, whether they involve people or situations, we have to find ways to replace them with positive thoughts that make us feel good and empowered. For example, if it's a dark and rainy day, I can choose to think about all the flowers that will soon bloom instead of complaining about how gloomy it is.

Of course, you may have to take some tiny baby steps to change attitudes or beliefs you've held over a lifetime. One such baby step is to ask yourself a basic question: "What can I visualize that could achieve a positive outcome?"

This should be kept simple and the goal should be realistic. It can even be confined to a single interaction with another person, such as calling someone close to you out of the blue to tell them you love them and are thinking about them. Maybe this someone is your sister, and every time you call her, you end up disagreeing about something and the interaction quickly degenerates into a screaming battle.

Trick her. Call her and say, "I was thinking about you and I love you." Then change the pattern by hanging up. When everyone else is zigging, choose to zag. Where there was negativity, try a completely opposite behavior.

See what happens, and pay close attention to how it makes you feel. Does it make you giggle, smile, feel better about life?

I think that people by and large discount the small acts of kindness, caring, and compassion that can magically change the energy around them. For example, I'm a firm believer that we cannot say "Thank you" too much. Likewise, I try to always be kind to those who work in restaurants and make them feel good versus always looking for something to be irritated about. Just the simple act of giving a compliment to a woman about her shoes makes her smile, and I smile in return.

Gratitude also goes a long way. I woke up this morning, climbed out of bed, got dressed, and drove myself to my office. After work, I had the luxury of being able to go out to eat. I have so many choices about the things I want, and I'm not going to let my day be ruined because some minute detail doesn't go my way. Everyone experiences an upward spiral and a downward spiral, and we each get to choose how we respond. We can be grateful, or we can complain. Step away from negativity for an hour, a day, or a week and see how different it makes you feel.

Choose to surround yourself with non-toxic people. Misery loves company, and people who are miserable love you to be just like them. Realize that you are making a choice to hang out with that SOB who does nothing but complain about everything. It can be as easy as a few clicks on the computer to find a community of people whose interests can spark something positive and uplifting in you. Our ability to give, share, and receive help and support makes us feel connected and empowered and can replace the fear, dread, and isolation that dominate so much of our spirit.

Exercising generosity of spirit and giving to others is one of the biggest highs we can experience. When asked what they're most proud of, famous and wealthy people overwhelmingly cite deeds of philanthropy, but you don't have to be wealthy to be philanthropic. Even the smallest gesture of kindness can be a tonic to your spirit.

In my own case, nothing can hold a candle to the joy I experienced several years ago when I took my parents to look at a new house under construction down the street. It was their fiftieth wedding anniversary, and I had made a special trip home to see them.

"Show me that house they're building," I suggested to my parents as we drove down the street. "There's an open house sign outside. Let's stop and take a look."

My father was game, but my mother was reluctant.

"There's no sense in doing that. We can't afford it," she said.

"Let's walk around inside," I suggested after coaxing them out of the car.

"What's the point?" my mother continued. "I'm never going to live in this house."

We walked inside. A fire was crackling in the fireplace. My mother touched the draperies, admiring the quality. I finally got them to sit on the couch in the living room.

"Do you think you could live in a house like this?" I asked.

"Hell, yeah," my father blurted out.

"Well, you're going to," I told them, "because it's yours."

When it finally sank in, my parents burst out crying. (They had missed a clue on our tour of the house—the towels in the bathroom were monogrammed with their initials.)

Many months before, I had purchased the empty lot and started construction. For a year, my father had been telling me, "They're building a house down the street, and you know, it has a detached garage!" This was his dream.

It was another three months before they moved in, but all they needed to take with them were their toothbrushes. My father was overjoyed that he finally had a place with a garage after living in row houses his whole life.

This was a big relief to me, because my parents, like most people of their generation in the lower middle class, never want anything given to them. They want to take care of themselves. My parents still feel a little funny about the house, but now I couldn't pry them out of there with a crowbar. As for me, the act of giving it to them remains the happiest experience of my life.

Just like the power of prayer I mentioned in the last chapter, I also believe firmly in the power of positive affirmations. My fitness trainer nailed it when he told me, "Change your focus, change your future." He may have

"This house is yours!"

been talking about achieving my goal of being healthy and fit, but this applies to everything else I do, too.

Look at yourself in the mirror and say, "I can make a change. I can be happy. I can work towards a solution."

If everything in your life is "I can't, I can't, I can't," then nothing is going to change. *You* have to change. Even if you are only able to move the needle one degree to a more positive reading, you will begin to see results.

In the affirmation department, I'm almost embarrassed to admit I do something really silly whenever I feel worn out or am harboring anger and resentment. Whether I'm in the shower or at the gym at the end of the day, I suddenly break into song. Not just any song, but a Disney song, the theme song from the children's movie *Frozen* called "Let It Go." Picture this, a fifty-some-year-old guy on a treadmill belting out:

> *Let it go, let it go,*
> *Can't hold me back anymore.*
> *Let it go, let it go,*
> *Turn away and slam the door.*
> *Here I stand and here I stay,*
> *Let the storm rage on.*
> *The cold never bothered me anyway.*

My fellow fitness enthusiasts get not just one chorus but the full rendition, word for word, from start to finish. What's even more remarkable is that the louder I sing, the better it seems to work. The people on the other treadmills

"Let it go!"

may think, "Who's that crazy man?" but I've never received a negative comment. Most of the time, they just smile. It makes me smile back, and the next thing I know, I really have let it go, whatever "it" is.

On a more serious note, one basic but highly effective way to root out negative influences in my life is to sit down and make a list of the pros and cons of a particular issue or behavior. Before making a decision about anything, I look at all the bad things I might be facing and then go to the opposite side of the continuum and consider all the good things I see. If the balance sheet shows that the disadvantages hover around 50% or greater, it's time to think about eliminating or replacing the issue or behavior.

Finally, I want to emphasize the power and importance of forgiveness, especially self-forgiveness. When we are younger, we are prone to do stupid things and not understand the nature of cause and effect. As a child, I had a habit of moving my knee joint in and out, making an annoying "boom-boom, boom-boom" sound. In school, I earned plenty of attention from doing this because it was really loud. Frankly, it irritated the hell out of people. My mother would yell at me, "You need to stop that; it's gross!" My father would add his own two cents: "Don't do that, because when you get old, it's not going to be good for you. You'll regret it."

Sure enough, I developed knee problems. Now when I'm around kids who are doing stupid things, I say the same things to them about regretting it when they're older, not that they pay any more attention than I did. "Hey, you really need to put that sunblock on," I once told a kid at the pool. "I'll worry about that when I'm old like you," he snapped back.

As we age, our mistakes bring even greater consequences and greater regrets. We let our credit card debt soar. We don't sink that extra $3,000 each year into our IRA account. We spend money we should have saved chasing the wrong relationship. We think of how our lives would be different if we hadn't messed up. Hindsight is always 20/20.

It's a very powerful achievement to be able to forgive ourselves and others for mistakes and transgressions, both those we cause and those that are inflicted upon us. When we can achieve this, we can begin to drop the clutter, get rid of the confusion, develop a plan, and focus on improvement.

Nonetheless, it seems like it's built into our DNA to remember pain, specifically the pain we feel and less so the pain we cause others. Many times, those who hurt us completely forget what they've done or simply rationalize it as not a big deal. But we remember the pain. Just like we quickly learn not to put our hand into the flame on the kitchen stove, our minds create ingenious ways to avoid any and all stimuli that might remind us of the pain and hurt we once experienced. Sometimes this goes as far back as early childhood, when our conscious memories erase pain we endured.

On the other hand, our inability to forgive ourselves and others and our resulting pain, disappointment, and anger can paralyze us and prevent us from experiencing joy and happiness at our core. Joy and happiness are often associated with the superficial. After all, it's much easier to fake being happy than it is to fake being sad. It takes a lot more work (and saps a lot more energy) to be sad and depressed than it does to be happy.

This part of the process isn't easy and can be very tricky because of our instinctive efforts to avoid pain. The process of forgiveness may require us to play graphic home movies in our minds and re-live deep emotions and trauma that have long been stuffed down with a tight-fitting lid. I'm not a psychologist or a therapist, but I recognize how important it is to have someone to talk to, whether it's a good friend, a spiritual advisor, or a mental health professional who makes you feel safe and supported.

Regarding mental health, I want to bring a few thoughts out into the open. All of us have seen firsthand how stuck people can be if they're in a deep depression or some other state that is making them unbearably miserable. In that state, we are often unreceptive to the most mundane commonsense advice, let alone capable of taking charge of some of the critical, far-reaching issues this book addresses.

Yet even today, in spite of all the awareness we have that diseases and disorders of the mind are medical conditions just like cancer or kidney failure, there is still a stigma associated with them. When the chemicals in our minds create major disturbances that keep us from making sound choices, we need to get professional help. I have seen people respond very well to medications like Prozac and Cymbalta when prescribed and taken properly. These are obviously not long-term fixes, but they can help break the downward cycle. Still, people are reluctant to accept the fact that mental illnesses are on par with physical ones. They need to accept that it's okay to consult with a physician or therapist who specializes in these disorders. If individuals judge you for saying "I can't get out of this depression; I'm going to see if a doctor can help me," they aren't real friends who truly love and care about you.

I am very blessed to have a wise and dear friend to talk to when times are tough. We often pick up the phone and call each other to discuss what we're going through. After the call, I always feel better. Even if I don't come away with a resolution, I feel better because I've shared my fears and anxieties with someone. Thankfully, few individuals are truly isolated. The people we associate with may not have the same exact fears that we do, but everyone is more or less going through the same thing in trying to figure out our mortal coil.

Finally, one small exercise I use to help me move forward is to make another list. In one column, I list all my successes. In another, I list all my failures. Then I give myself praise for one and forgiveness for the other. Finally, I close with gratitude for everything I've learned through both. And, if I feel like it, I hum a few bars of "Let It Go."

Try it yourself. If changing your focus truly does mean changing your future, you have nothing to lose.

Chapter 6

The Amazing Eat-Less-Move-More Diet Breakthrough

Next on my list of prerequisites for a life of greater vitality as I grow older is something that is staring right back at me in the mirror.

Truth be told, there is nothing more devastating to our health and well-being than the stressful effects of being overweight. Try carrying around 40 or 50 pounds of extra cargo in a backpack while going about your everyday chores. See how it feels after a few minutes. Then go ahead and double the weight.

Welcome to a reality check on the horrendous toll obesity takes.

Some years back, the television show *MADtv* presented a painfully true but very funny sketch on the topic featuring comedian Crista Flanagan. Padded up to fit into a plus-plus-plus size dress, Ms. Flanagan bantered with an off-screen voice like you might hear in a commercial or infomercial, talking about a revolutionary new weight loss craze called Eat Less Move More. "It's too complicated," she complained. "Isn't there a pill I can take? It sounds like a scam you do to older persons," she added.

Although she said she wanted to lose weight, Ms. Flanagan found expedient and painfully recognizable excuses for why she couldn't do it. The skit ended by fading into another commercial for a box of Oreo-like cookies that Ms. Flanagan's character predictably tore into and devoured with relish.

The irony is, it really is as simple as it sounds: eat less and move more. The question is, why is it so difficult to do this? Overwhelming scientific research demonstrates that diet and exercise are at the top of the list of the most essential factors impacting our quality of life and longevity as we age. They rank even higher than quitting smoking. Not only does exercise make us look and feel better but losing weight and getting fit are a proven defense against heart attacks, strokes, diabetes, and a host of other chronic diseases and inflammatory conditions. In fact, staying fit is the number one best way to preserve your independence. Ask yourself which you would rather do: go to the gym and cut back on calories or go to the hospital/convalescent home? (Or, worse yet, take a premature one-way trip to the cemetery?)

There are really no good excuses for not exercising. Even if you are already compromised from a physical health standpoint, there are still highly effective exercises you can do while sitting in a chair or even in bed.

It is uplifting to see seniors who face obvious physical challenges making the effort to go to the gym. If you talk to them, they will tell you what a difference exercise makes. Even when we're elderly, the human body still has many remarkable healing and restorative powers. Once we get started, there's usually an immediate and tangible improvement. A movement that was difficult one day is easier the next. After a few days, you might be able to walk up a flight of stairs whereas before you had to stop due to shortness of breath. Suddenly you can even bend over to tie your shoes without strain or pain.

One geriatric sports medicine professor used to show her audience a slide of an extremely well trained and buff male torso. The man's physique looked good enough to be on the cover of *Men's Fitness* or *GQ*. The next slide made everyone gasp in surprise. It showed the same man in full frame, revealing the grizzled and wrinkled head of an eighty-year-old atop that manly torso. The point these photos make is that it's possible to maintain that kind of elite muscle tone and body fitness almost indefinitely as long you do the work and keep it up.

It must be extremely frustrating for that professor or any doctor or physical therapist to know that so many of the problems their patients face could be resolved with a variation of that extraordinary Eat Less Move More diet. The first step is getting off the couch and getting into motion (and not just walking over to a box of donuts in the kitchen).

Understanding the reasons the vast majority of us are resigned to a far less healthy status quo would probably require a session or two with a psychologist. There are no doubt genetic predispositions and metabolic factors that impact our individual obesity problems, but many of us do absolutely nothing to lessen our odds and instead mindlessly numb ourselves with our unhealthy food addictions. These behaviors and habits do a lot to hasten our horrible outcomes.

All it takes to get a sobering reality check is to visit a supermarket and check out what's piled up in the vast majority of shopping carts—sugary snacks, ice cream, soft drinks and alcohol, potato chips, unhealthy fats, and overly processed foods full of dubious additives. Countless millions also eat one or more meals daily at fast food restaurants. After the sugar, refined carbs, and salt rushes subside, they crash into a vicious cycle of feeling fatigued and unwell and are hardly capable of getting off the sofa, much less going for a walk or to the gym.

I'm certainly no angel in this regard, but I've decided not to focus on deprivation or abstinence but rather on balance. I view that list of offenders as treats and not the main fare. I also think, rightfully or wrongly, that if I throw in some green leafy vegetables and healthy fruit and go to the gym, I can still indulge—in moderation—in my sinful Häagen Dazs and other treats.

Exercising portion control (the "eat less" part) is key to any success. Defy the internalized voice of your mother telling you to "clean your plate." Start cutting back, and resist seconds.

No doubt many of us who neglect to eat healthy foods and get exercise are so used to the malaise of being unwell that we've grown to accept it as normal. It also doesn't help that if there's some bio-medical intervention that might cure or improve our condition, the fear of the white coat keeps many away.

I am sure my own mother knows deep down that her own very serious weight problem is a ticking time bomb. It certainly imposes real limits on what she can and cannot do. Efforts to get her to make changes always hit a wall of bricks and reinforced concrete. Since her only true form of exercise is playing Farmville, I offered to have a physical therapist come to the house to work with her. She refused. I tried to get her to go to the aqua-aerobics place a block away from her home. She didn't want anyone to see her in her bathing suit, and she didn't want to mess up her hair.

"I can get you a nice bathing suit and pay for you to get your hair done," I implored. "Or you could wear a pair of shorts and a t-shirt." When that got nowhere, I suggested she wear her girdle and pretend it was a bathing suit.

"I'm not getting in the pool in a girdle," she snapped, and that was the end of that.

I then took a different tact and had a dietician come see her. This woman began talking to my mom about do's and don'ts and then wanted to go through all her cabinets to remove everything that wasn't good for her. My mother promptly asked the woman to leave.

"I don't want anyone coming in here and telling me what I can have in my cupboards," she said.

"Mom, do you want help?"

"Yes, but I don't want anyone telling me what I have to do."

"You're not going to get help if you're not willing to accept that someone might know something you don't."

None of us can escape cause and effect, whether it comes to doing our homework, preparing to give a presentation, or losing weight. If we're unwilling to put the work in, nothing is going to change. We simply have to eat less and do more, preferably in combination.

Chapter 7

The Case for Doing Your Own Funeral Pre-Planning

T he next big challenge before us is to chip away at the fear of our own mortality. As I've indicated, this is the single biggest reason so many of us are members of what I call "The Retirement Crisis Club" (bigger by far than AARP). Death is always around us, so we don't have to scratch far below the surface to get up close and personal. Once we choose to engage instead of run away, as my own little experiment in immersion therapy illustrates, we may discover the bark is worse than the bite.

"How can we help you in your time of loss?" asked the compassionate-sounding voice of the man who answered the phone at the funeral home.

"We haven't had our loss yet," I told him, and immediately I heard the light tapping of fingers on a keyboard as he quickly jumped to a different section of the prepared script on his computer screen.

There was an unfortunate necessity for me to make this call. My brother Tracy was in the final stages of his terminal illness, and I had told my parents not to worry, that I would handle the arrangements, so I was calling the local funeral home they'd suggested.

"We'll certainly provide services that will be most respectful to your loved one," the voice began. The man went on to talk about how long his funeral home had been around. He explained that its services were a staple of the community and began describing the various packages available to me. It was hard to not notice how frequently he repeated the word "respect," and not in that endearing Aretha Franklin kind of way.

"For you to show the most respect to your loved one, we would recommend the gladiator model." The man went into used car salesman mode, pitching the list of extra accessories in rapid fire. "Brass hardware…Silk liner with multiple colors to choose from…The seal is guaranteed for many years…." And so on.

"What is your least expensive model?" I interrupted. "I think I just want the basic one."

"Well, that one…" The tone in the salesman's voice was markedly less enthusiastic.

The aggressive attempt to upsell the coffin was hardly mysterious. Because coffins represent a sizeable profit center, corporate conglomeration has impacted the funeral home industry just as it has so many other industries. Many small, family-run funeral parlors have been systematically bought up by coffin manufacturers who market directly to consumers and thus eliminate the middleman. The funeral home I happened to be talking to was an exception to this trend and still family owned.

The conversation went on and on. "The standard is to have two days of viewing; that is the most acceptable. That gives you time for the grieving process. We can also select the music."

"How much is all that?" Trying to get a firm price out of him was like trying to extract a stubborn tooth, but then it got even more interesting. The man asked if my loved one had a life insurance policy. I told him Tracy did, albeit a small one; it was one of those $10,000 Gerber Baby policies my grandparents had bought when he was born.

"Wonderful. Bring the life insurance policy and assign it to us. We'll take care of everything. You'll still be responsible for any of the premiums, but, if not, we'll subtract that amount on the final invoice."

"How does that work?" I asked.

"So that you're not bothered at your time of grieving, we'll take the administrative burden of filing the life insurance policy for you."

"Where do the proceeds go?"

"We collect the proceeds for you. We subtract what we've spent and deliver any remainder to you."

Fat chance, I thought, and I promptly told the salesman that wouldn't be necessary. I was sure there wouldn't be any proceeds left once they figured out how much the policy was worth and finished tacking on all sorts of fees and expenses. All the pressure the salesman was putting on me made me realize just how vulnerable we are if we don't plan ahead, an impression that only grew in intensity as the process unfolded.

I decided to check out the competition and call another funeral home. Same process. Same script. Then I said, "The other place is doing it for X dollars."

"We'll beat that quote," I promptly heard. "Send me their quote."

Now I was playing funeral parlor poker. I have to confess, Tracy's imminent death aside, that I enjoyed the whole spectacle of them down-bidding to compete for my business.

Both salesmen wanted me to sign over Tracy's life insurance policy, which I was not going to do. They also wanted me to come in to see their facilities. I had been to both places at multiple funerals over the years, I told them.

"I think I just want the basic."

Ah, but had I been in their display rooms? No? Well, I had to go to the display room before anything was finalized so I could see samples of the different coffins and fixtures.

Both agents had me sign forms with representations and warranties that my consumer rights and options had been adequately presented and explained, a red flag that the industry's prior policies and practices have aroused regulatory hackles and need cleaning up.

Then I had to call the cemetery where my parents had bought plots to begin another negotiation. The fee for opening the grave was $2,000; this was the price for the basic hole in the ground. I held myself back from asking if I could bring my own backhoe and dig it myself. If I wanted Astroturf carpet trimming to hide the dirt, that was an extra cost. Did I want a covered canopy? A carpet walkway from which the family car would let me out? What about umbrellas in case of rain?

Here again came the sales pitch with that ultimate guilt-inducing phrase—"to show your ultimate respect to your loved one." Like the deceased was going to be walking around saying, "You only had fifteen chairs? You should have had twenty," or "Why did you pick green Astroturf? I wanted red."

The follow-up meeting at the cemetery happened in a special space that was dedicated to displaying headstone varieties, and aggressively so, in the same way as the funeral home's casket extravaganza. I could get my loved one's facial mask sculpted in bronze and mounted to the stone. I could get a three-dimensional photographic image of my loved one embedded in rock. If I wanted to go ultra deluxe, I could opt for a memorial bench and, better yet, a stone vault. In response, I told the salesman I wasn't interested in a headstone or anything else right now and would get back to him at a later date.

Planning the viewing and wake for my brother also brought forth the agonizing question about whether to have an open or closed casket, another trauma-inducing choice and an extra cost to consider. With the open casket, you usually have a lot of people standing around saying things like "He looks like he's asleep" or "She's finally at peace."

I can't help but ask, do you think it's important for people to actually see your loved one's corpse? Is it a way to make sure the whole thing isn't a hoax, even if everyone knew the person was dying? Is the point to make everyone lose it and cry?

One extreme in this area that you may have heard about is how some have the viewing staged and choreographed to show the deceased engaged in his or her favorite activity. One man was famously buried in a special coffin so he could ride his Harley for eternity. My vote is that a nicely framed picture and a closed casket are the way to go!

In fact, this experience confirmed for me that there was no reason I shouldn't go ahead and plan my own arrangements in advance. I certainly didn't want to leave this burden for my loved ones or anybody else. How could they know for certain what I might want? Chances are they'd fall for the "respect" pitch and do more rather than less, whether out of guilt, embarrassment, grief, or a combination of all three.

At least my brother Tracy had the opportunity to weigh in on the plans for his services. He was adamant that he wanted to be buried wearing his beloved leather jacket, the one embellished on the back with the photo of that berserk Jack Nicholson character in *The Shining* holding the ax and shouting "Here's Johnny!"

Tracy no doubt identified with the character's frustration and the madness that resulted from not being able to achieve what he set out to do in life. Tracy's downward spiral began his senior year of high school. The high point of his life was being the quarterback of his football team. The coach pushed him too much, putting more and more pressure on him, and Tracy began to crack. He probably had more than one concussion from playing, too, which we now know can create lingering lifelong problems. Decades of alcohol and substance abuse followed, and the consequences of all the health complications hastened his early death.

I overheard an argument between my parents not long before Tracy died. "We're not having all those football trophies in the casket," my father barked. "But that's what he wants," my mother countered. Along with the leather jacket, Tracy wanted those mementos, and he also requested that his coffin be painted Wolverine green, the color of his football team's uniform.

The final arrangement to think about was where to hold his wake. "Should we have it here at home?" my parents wondered.

I envisioned everyone somberly hovering over the dining room table eating cold cuts from a deli platter. I proposed instead renting out the hall at my brother's home away from home, a bar called the Commodore. I suggested we have a bull roast, a traditional Maryland way to celebrate anything with draft beer and pit beef with a deejay.

"That isn't a wake," my parents protested.

"Why isn't it a wake?" I countered.

Once they got their heads around the idea, something remarkable happened. The shroud of scariness over the whole thing lifted. Planning a bull roast for Tracy altered what would certainly be a sad and morose gathering into a celebration of his life. Even Tracy, who loved bull roasts, signed off on it from his sick bed, saying, "Yeah, that's something I would really like."

And guess what? When the time came, it was far better than we ever could have imagined. As strange as it may sound, the whole affair turned out to be remarkably pleasant. First of all, the same hard-sell people at the funeral home could not have been more thoughtful and professional to deal with and handled all the details with the utmost dignity and grace. (Maybe my no-nonsense approach during the pre-planning told them I wasn't one to play around with and scared them into being on their best behavior.) I was also pleasantly surprised at how good

Tracy looked in the coffin, better than he'd looked in the last years of his life, with his hair cut, clean shaven, and in a nice suit.

The bull roast turned out to be just the huge and empowering celebration of his life that we wanted it to be. The songs the deejay played set the right mood. Speeches were made against the backdrop of enlarged photos of Tracy. Many of the guests picked from the sunflowers that decorated the room and placed them in their empty Budweiser bottles to create their own makeshift memorials. An astounding sight was watching my parents slow dance to "Under the Boardwalk." It must have been decades since they'd graced a dance floor. They even finished the moment by giving each other a kiss.

The only off-putting element in the whole thing was the handwritten note of condolence a few days later from the headstone salesman, who also inserted his business card.

I don't know if this story will inspire you to go out and plan your own funeral, but it sure inspired me. My thought was, "Why not do it now?" Once you know you're in the active stages of dying, it may be a bit too late to do it with a clear mind. You may be far too absorbed in what Elizabeth Kübler Ross called the five stages of death and dying: denial, anger, bargaining, depression, and finally, acceptance. Her pioneering work that inspired the hospice movement was controversial when it came out in the late 1960s. Some colleges refused to teach or even discuss her theories. While her philosophy was a good start toward promoting better understanding and dialogue about death and dying, it was ultimately flawed because it didn't acknowledge the dying process until it was in full swing, when it was too late to pre-plan to circumvent or reduce some of the more unfortunate consequences.

Despite arranging Tracy's funeral and planning my own, I'm not saying I've conquered all my fears and phobias about death and dying. All it takes to make me shudder while getting on my next flight is for three hundred people to go down in an airplane disaster. The way I fly around on planes, its really gets to me. "It can't happen to me," I say to myself. Best to put it out of mind and move on.

If you're thinking about planning your own final arrangements, one of the first steps you might consider is taking out funeral insurance. Depending on the costs, this might be a good thing. It really isn't insurance but more of a prepaid plan, almost like purchasing on layaway (no pun intended). Once you take this first action, it's much easier to move forward on other important decisions on the planning checklist.

Doing my own funeral pre-planning has given me a profound sense of relief. I certainly don't want others playing funeral parlor poker on my behalf, nor do I want them making the decision about whether my coffin lid will be open or shut (*shut!*).

Instead, I've been very detailed in my instructions to leave no stone unturned (especially the headstone). I feel empowered by this planning because I want some say in my final send-off. The few variables I've left in are designed

Chapter 8

Downsizing and Feeling Really Good about It

nother demon that literally stands in the way of our progress is the clutter that clogs our lives in the form of material possessions that pile up without serving any meaningful purpose. Making matters worse, our addiction to acquiring stuff means we add to this burdensome collection by acquiring more things we don't really need.

A recent report stated that modern Americans are so addicted to stuff that our individual possessions are far greater than the sum of all the combined possessions of our ancestors going back many generations. Not a surprise, and one good reason why the self-storage business is thriving.

If there's a section of the book I personally need to take seriously, this is it. Like many Americans, one of the hardest things to corral is my constant urge to continuously buy things, but there are countless reasons why it's prudent and healthy to rein in our over-consumption, especially of items that aren't truly essential.

With that goal in mind, it's vitally important for each of us to begin examining our spending habits, because even the greatest planning advice for securing our financial future will go out the window if we're out of control with our credit cards.

Nonetheless, I'm the kind of person who sees a sale, buys something on credit, and then convinces himself he's saved enough to pay it off. If I wander around a mall, there's a better than even chance I'll walk out with some shiny new gadget or maybe a polo shirt to add to the dozen I already have. I tell myself, "Oh, I need that!" My mind acts like a child begging for candy at the supermarket checkout. I'm sure some of my compulsive behavior is a result of boredom, but there are no doubt deeper things going on.

For me, and for many of us, walking out of a store with a shopping bag is like getting a fix. It makes the endorphins fly. This phenomenon is well known by cable television home shopping networks. They know the triggers and profit by the millions of dollars to be made preying on the addictive chemistry of the impulse buy.

What I personally need is a cooling off period, similar to when you purchase firearms, to defuse my impulsive actions. Sometimes, taking a deep breath, I tell myself, "Discipline! I'm going to cut back on luxuries I don't need. I'm not going to go out this weekend. I'm going to eat at home."

If this fails and I'm confronted with a possible new purchase, I go down my three vital checklist questions: "Is this something I need to have at this very moment? Is this going to keep me alive or help someone I love? What is the result of me not having this object?" Then I give myself more assurance: "Nothing is going to change over the next 24 hours. Why not go home and sleep on it?" Chances are I'll come to my senses and realize I don't need this item or to spend this money after all.

I can even go a step further and look at my potential new acquisitions as they correlate to Maslow's hierarchy of needs. This is a highly useful and wonderful breakdown of mostly beneficial human aspirations formulated by psychologist Abraham Maslow in the 1940s.

Maslow described a pyramid starting at the base with physiological needs (breathing, food, water, sex, sleep) and progressing upwards to include safety (security of body, employment, family, health, property), love/belonging (friendship, family, sexual intimacy), esteem (self-esteem, confidence, achievement, respect), and self-actualization (morality, creativity, spontaneity, problem solving).

It's a nice litmus test to hold any impending purchase of material goods or services against Maslow's pyramid to judge whether or not it will positively impact your health, well-being, and human potential.

Perhaps the worst and most costly manifestation of stupid consumption comes from playing the fool's game of trying to impress others. Here again, I bring a personal tale of woe.

In the early 2000s, I built a contemporary *Architectural Digest*-worthy home in Ft. Lauderdale, Florida. Everything was custom-this and custom-that. Red Italian leather wrapped the fireplace and the stairway banister. The floors were made of the finest teak and marble and repeated on the outside decking (this quickly became a maintenance nightmare). Even my private dock, from which I could watch million-dollar yachts float by on the Las Olas Intercoastal Waterway, was made of teak. The open floor plan allowed the onyx-sculptured wet bar in the living room to seamlessly morph into the kitchen counter at its opposite end.

In the bedroom, I had a refrigerator/freezer built into my bedside table so I could conveniently reach my stash of Häagen Dazs without having to get up. Similarly, smart home technology allowed me with the push of a button to lower the shades, adjust the air conditioner, turn on the pool heater, and engage the security system. Except, somehow, every time I pushed one of those buttons, it seemed like something broke. In retrospect, this was a bad omen of things to come.

I couldn't wait to have my housewarming party on New Year's Eve so as many people as possible could come and exclaim, "Oh my God; this is incredible!" I had told the architect I wanted a "wow" around every corner, and he had succeeded.

As if the house weren't "wow" enough, I pulled out all the stops for the big event, enlisting a company to install special lighting and bring in high tables for the deck to hold cocktails. All this stupid stuff would prove I had "made it" and would compel people to look at me with admiration.

Needless to say, it blew up in my face. I wanted people to be happy for me, but it didn't work out that way. The teachable moment was that just because you have something special you're proud of it doesn't mean everyone else is going to feel that way.

To be frank, my efforts turned friends off. I came off as a braggart. I also became an easy target for people who don't like to see others succeed. Some even made a point of going around to find something that wasn't "wow." I was told, "You should have changed those knobs. They aren't special enough." The party became a celebration of jealousy, bitterness, condemnation, and negativity. Playing it back, how pretentious it all was, yet what the hell was I doing? Had I been a guest at that party, I probably wouldn't have liked me, either.

In the interests of full disclosure, I was trying to impress someone. It didn't work, and that person no doubt soon forgot about my misguided efforts and moved on to more pressing concerns. The fact is, other people have a whole host of problems that we don't see behind their perfectly manicured lawns and the beautiful shiny cars parked in front of their mansions. There's no telling what personal and financial dramas are going on behind closed doors, well beyond our superficial judgments of them. What we need to do is take a good look at what we're doing to ourselves.

It's a pretty good bet that neither my party nor my house left a lasting impression on the Joneses or any of my other friends and acquaintances, or if it did, it went something like, "Gee, what an idiot!"

To add insult to injury, after investing a small fortune in this house, I lost it all in the housing crash of 2008. My New Year's Eve housewarming party, so carefully designed with my grandiose materialism on display to show that I had arrived, actually foreshadowed the complete opposite—my financial demise!

I learned in the process that I didn't need to live in a palatial space. Instead, real life and what mattered most to my happiness took place in the cozier, more intimate, confines like the kitchen (where food was prepared and eaten, TV watched, and most conversations had) and the bedroom. The other rooms in this over-the-top masterpiece proved totally useless and horribly unnecessary.

In becoming older and wiser, I learned, too, that many of the people I was trying to impress proved to be the garden variety of fair-weather friend. They were always there if a party invitation or free drinks or dinner were being offered, but I learned not to hold my breath for any reciprocal gestures. And a warning: if you happen to be going through a period of economic downturn as I was for a couple of years after losing the house, such "friends" will disappear from your life faster than rats from a sinking ship.

On the other hand, this experience taught me to value and treasure the close core of true friends who stayed with me through thick and thin and who love me, warts and all. No doubt this is why some Native American tribes, before the Europeans came, based their wealth on the number of enriching personal relationships they had and not on any notion of individual material wealth.

I'll admit I'm not yet completely free from my addiction to conspicuous consumption. Again, I refer back to my explanation (excuse) about being "a work in progress." At the moment, I'm at a crossroads with the whole automobile thing. I'm driving a big BMW 750. Recently, I was doing some business coaching for a friend who wanted to buy a new car for his business travel, and we were calculating the pros and cons of getting a hybrid. This got me thinking about my own situation. I really don't need this giant gas-guzzling machine. I no doubt bought it as a status symbol, so people would see me driving and say, "Wow, that guy is really accomplished and successful!"

The hybrid car is functionally the same thing as my BMW, designed to move me about comfortably. If I'm still interested in sending a message by a public display of my possessions, at least driving a hybrid would be a comparatively more forward-thinking and environmentally conscious statement.

When it comes to making decisions about downsizing significant financial possessions or obligations, the same process of asking critical questions applies: do I need it? Why am I buying it/keeping it? Is it for me or is it to impress someone? Does it cover my basic needs? Can I really afford it?

One of the most agonizing questions many of us will face, assuming we haven't already, is whether or not to sell the family home. While I will discuss more practical considerations later on, let's focus on the behavioral aspect first. The rationale most often put forward for holding onto the old house is as misguided and delusional as building my ill-fated palace in Florida. When I talk to people going through this difficult decision, many act as though letting the family house go means they'll lose their memories. Even more irrational is the belief that keeping the house somehow means those memories will be recaptured or relived, like trying to restage the happy memory of a family holiday gathering when the children were small. No matter what you do, you are doomed to futility, unless you happen to have a machine capable of time travel.

The whole idea of downsizing and getting off the consumer merry-go-round flies in the face of some of our deepest and most complicated personal attachments, but these attachments are precisely what are so often counterproductive. Engaging in the process of asking ourselves if we truly need the things we feel compelled to buy or keep is tough to do in the heat of battle, but try. You'll experience soon enough just how considerable the rewards are for making this breakthrough.

Chapter 9

Encore Careers and Other Ways of Reinventing Yourself

I don't want to retire because then I'll have a fixed income," my father told me when the time came for him to give up his day job. "Whenever I needed extra money before, I could always work overtime or take a second job."

My father's worries are echoing across breakfast tables all over this country and indeed the world. With the per capita retirement savings per American household at a mere $3,000 according to the dismal forecast I referenced earlier, there is good reason to get creative with some innovative problem solving. As long as we're healthy enough to get out of bed and have the power of mind and body to function efficiently, this situation can be turned from one of high anxiety and demoralizing stress to one of greater joy and fulfillment.

"Dad, just because you're retiring doesn't mean you can't work and make money," I countered. Since my father had waited past full retirement age to claim his benefits, he could earn extra money without the kind of penalties he might have incurred had he filed at age 62 or subsequent years before his sixty-sixth birthday.

"You're a master welder," I reminded him. "You have valuable skills. Why can't you get a little trailer to put all your equipment in, make a few signs, and become a handyman?"

I had a similar conversation with a dear friend of mine who was leaving her job in the government as an accountant and auditor. She told me that she was retiring with a pension worth 75% of her current income but was still anxious about how she would be able to maintain her standard of living. While she was in a different economic stratosphere than my father, the same fix applied. Instead of hitching a trailer to her car, I suggested she go back to her former employer as a part-time contractor. Her income suddenly ballooned to 125% of her last paycheck!

The other thing people retiring from their day jobs don't always think about is the costs associated with their former 9:00 to 5:00 existence. If you don't have to go to a job every day, your expenses related to transportation, clothing, and food can be dramatically reduced. You no longer have to keep up appearances by buying more expensive cars or designer clothes and going to fancy restaurants, but why stop there? You can also scale down other big-ticket items, like that giant house you no longer need.

Leaving the demands of the 9:00 to 5:00 world behind also opens up a whole new world. You suddenly have the freedom to do the things that are important to you and can even develop new skill sets in areas where your true interests and passions lie. For example, if you love cross-stitching or growing orchids, why not do that for eight hours a day and earn some extra income by setting up a booth at the local flea market to sell your products? Why not go to school to become a master chef or further your passion for learning some other artisan skill? For that matter, if you love talking and interacting with people, what's so bad about being a Walmart greeter or working at an information desk at the local hospital or airport? Something extraordinarily magical happens when you stop working for money and start earning money from the things you enjoy.

Making these sorts of shifts is much easier if you have your affairs in a somewhat orderly state. Embracing change and getting creative is challenging if not impossible if you're worried about the unknowns and don't have a plan. I know that when I have a plan in place, I can relax and put myself out in the universe to both await and create new opportunities. Taking that first step and making those plans is key.

One of the more positive offshoots of the baby boomers' illusion that they will live forever is this embrace of expanded lifestyle choices that weren't possible a generation ago. Today's seniors are attracted to vibrant environments. They want to go out and live, now that they finally have time. Of course, it's obviously easier to live out your fantasies and move to a college town, Costa Rica, or Tuscany if you have the financial wherewithal plus decent health. Likewise, if you don't have half a million dollars in your retirement piggy bank, such grandiose plans will remain a pipe dream.

If you do have the ability to move, give thought to the fact that there are plenty of locations where the cost of living is more affordable than Miami Beach, Santa Barbara, or the Hamptons. Research smaller towns and cities and rural areas that have good healthcare services, even if they don't come to mind first as the hippest places to relocate. According to a recently published survey, few of the 10 most affordable places to retire are on most Americans' radar screens. These include small towns like Decatur, Alabama; Clarksville, Tennessee; Corpus Christi, Texas; Alexandria, Louisiana; and Aiken, South Carolina, plus larger cities like Pittsburgh, Indianapolis, Tampa, Tulsa, and Omaha. These locations not only have lower living costs (taxes, home prices, and the cost of goods and services) but also factor in weather, attractions, and quality healthcare.

If you are considering moving, here are some things to consider:

1. The weather. In other words, do you like it hot or cold? Personally, I wouldn't move anywhere that gets frigid. Atlanta, where I live right now, is the perfect climate for me.

2. The dynamics. Do you thrive on the energy of other people? You don't have to choose Manhattan, but do consider a location that has a lot to offer— think culture, museums, and/or a college-like environment. Again, I love Atlanta. Emery and Georgia Tech are nearby, plus it has great sporting events, wonderful restaurants, beautiful parks and gardens, and lots of nice things to do, many of which are free.

3. Accessibility. Don't live in an isolated, hard-to-reach region. Make it easy for people to come see you. A lot of us are not going to want to travel as we get older. Airports and sardine-can seating on planes can be joyless. Don't move somewhere that requires a dozen connections and a bus ride or else you're going to sit there and be mad that no one comes to visit. Also make sure there are good healthcare services nearby.

4. Cost of living. Do some research and make sure this location is affordable. Take stock of what your needs are and whether you have a support system in place (like nearby family members

who can help when necessary) that can reduce your costs.

In a variation of moving, one of my favorite ideas to consider is co-housing. Not long ago, on one of my regular appearances to talk retirement issues on the Fox Business Channel, I decided to float the concept of co-housing that first came on the radar thanks to the *Golden Girls* television sitcom. I explained that due to the high divorce rate and the rise in unconventional American family structures, many boomers facing the prospect of retiring alone are managing to maintain a vibrant and enjoyable lifestyle by living with other singles in homes comparable to or better than the ones they shared with their spouses!

On live television, the host of the show, Stuart Varney, questioned me skeptically about whether people would really go for such an idea, but the immediate wave of response in social media said otherwise.

In my view, your family includes those you love and care about, not just those who share your bloodline. One of the most wonderful things about getting older is that lifelong friends can become close extended family who can indeed live together and support one another. When it works, such arrangements can be as dynamic and creative as more expensive and exotic environments.

In this set-up, each individual brings their life experiences and skills to the mix. One person might know how to bank well and can handle the finances. Maybe another person has a musical background and can entertain everyone by playing the piano. Another member might be a retired nurse or handyman. The point is, everyone pools their resources, lives together, and helps care for each other. Personally, I think it's brilliant.

Nonetheless, communal living arrangements can be tricky unless they're carefully planned. To be successful, expectations have to be set up front, and transparency is key. Think of it like a mini homeowners association with ground rules that everyone has to buy into and sign off on. Each member has to be upfront about their net worth and contribute what they can, even if it's pro-rated based on what they can afford.

In addition, everyone has to respect each other's boundaries. Conflicts will always arise; it's how they're resolved that matters. Open lines of communication, rational solutions, fairness, and equality—regardless of differing economic positions—are key. Maybe such homes should be run like a democracy in which everyone has a vote. For example, on Wednesday nights, everyone votes on whether to watch *Dancing with the Stars* or a rerun of *Dr. Quinn Medicine Woman*. Those who don't like the decision can choose to watch something else in their own room.

One last word of caution: I wouldn't advise anyone to jump into a co-housing arrangement without knowing his or her prospective roommates well and having a thorough conversation to make sure everyone is on the same page long before the idea is put into motion. Otherwise, you could wind up with a horrible reality show right in your living room, something along the lines of *Senior Survival*, with a plot that goes as follows: throw a bunch of old people together in a house and watch as they beat each other to death with canes and walkers.

On the other hand, if you know what to expect, and if you plan well enough to avoid the pitfalls, such an arrangement could be close to paradise.

Part 2

THE RIGHT TOOLS FOR THE RIGHT JOB

To recap, Part 1 confronted some deep-seated roadblocks that stand in the way of becoming older, wiser, and worry-free in our golden years. These fears, attachments, and other unhealthy attitudes and habits bear the lion's share of responsibility for the less than desirable straits so many seniors are facing.

This second section of the book looks at some of the most important options for improving our prospects in our old age and reveals key inside facts, knowledge that many corporations and service providers would prefer none of us to have. Understanding some of the tricks of the trade and what to watch out for makes it easier to navigate through these choices. With the right information, we can each become smart buyers rather than victims of slick, idealized sales presentations that leave out the less desirable realities or bury them in user agreements that few of us bother to read.

As I explained before, hundreds of books and websites provide detailed know-how on the vast complexities of the numerous financial planning strategies for old age.

This is one reason I purposely made this a shorter and more concise book. Wading through a lot of complex minutia that may or may not be relevant to your particular situation may induce sleep or cause you to relegate this book to that sad stack of unfinished works destined for the yard sale.

Instead, almost everything I talk about concerns quality of life issues that will arise with absolute certainty for you as well as your friends and loved ones. As you know by now, making better informed decisions and doing so sooner rather than later can have enormous, even life-saving, consequences.

To repeat, once you accept the reality of old age and death with a less fear-based attitude, you will be able to exercise the full might of your intellect, wisdom, and judgment and not be subject to emotional, knee-jerk, and impulsive reactions because you ventured outside your comfort zone.

Here's one example: some of us will eventually consider getting a reverse mortgage on our homes to help meet our expenses. What's more, this may prove to be a great solution. However, if you're feeling desperate and emotionally vulnerable, you will probably be focused on closing the deal and getting money in your hands as quickly as possible. This may prevent you from having the forethought to ask if your spouse can stay in the home for the rest of his or her life if you die first or whether there's a possibility he or she might become homeless. Government regulations have stepped in to clean up a lot of abuses like this example, but there are still a good many pitfalls to avoid, as I'll discuss in greater detail later.

If you're ready to read about some of these tools that can help you make the best possible decisions for yourself and your family, turn the page and let's begin.

Chapter 10

Retirement Income Calculators

Almost every financial institution including banks, insurance companies, brokerage houses, and even our government offers on-line calculators designed to help us get a handle on our income, create a budget, and help us make better decisions. No doubt many of us with fear-based, avoidance mentalities have not taken advantage of this tool, thinking, "What's the point? It's just going to confirm my worst fears."

Again, my goal is to dismantle the fear of the unknown and replace it with information and empowerment. Used with the right mindset, these calculators can be very useful in helping set realistic goals and coming up with innovative strategies to bridge any gaps.

Many of the calculators found online are quite good. In a perfect world, I would recommend one of the government-sponsored sites, but as many Americans recently experienced in the Obamacare software debacle, not much thought is usually given to making interfaces user-friendly and easy to navigate. (One exception I recently discovered is the Social Security Administration's website.) Many of the corporate sponsored sites are fine, but they obviously want to lead you to buy a product or services from them, so proceed with caution. On the other hand, websites run by non-profit organizations may have a more neutral, less self-serving agenda. As mentioned earlier, visit www.ScottPage.com for my list of recommended calculators.

What most of these calculators have in common is the ability to help you set up a basic budget. They ask simple questions, such as how much income you have or will have from Social Security, if you are going to work, and if so, what earnings you will receive. They ask what you have in savings and investments and also ask you to list all your bills. After crunching the numbers, they tell you the cold hard truth of what you have to work with.

In the absence of this knowledge lurks the kind of financial stress that can be devastating and can stop you in your tracks just as easily as some of the other roadblocks I've discussed.

Remember Mr. Micawber's famous recipe for happiness in Charles Dickens' novel *David Copperfield*? "Annual income twenty pounds, annual expenditure nineteen pounds, nineteen shillings and six pence, result happiness. Annual income twenty pounds, annual expenditure twenty pounds ought and six, result misery."

Thanks to the debacle of my "wow" house, I know intimately of what Mr. Micawber speaks, having swung back and forth from being on the brink of losing everything to later having disposable income based on 25 years of running a company. I've learned from my past mistakes and have a solid plan in place, but I talk to people every day who are facing financial difficulties. Whether they are $250 short or their budget deficit is a hundred times that and they are at risk of losing their homes, I can hear in their voices how stressed out they are. Worry and stress take the same toll, no matter how many zeroes you add to the problem.

Running the numbers on one of these calculators may give you a bit of an unpleasant shock. It might spit back at you what you already suspected—that you can't maintain your current standard of living for the rest of your life. Rather than getting demoralized and sticking your self-pitying head back in the sand, accept the reality that you need to make some adjustments. After all, these calculators are not the final word, just a friendly warning telling you what will happen if you do nothing.

The worst thing you can do is close your eyes to the situation. You need to open up to constructive changes and get into forward motion, chipping away at the shortfall. It might be a good time to consider some of the downsizing strategies I discuss in this book. Sell the house or get a reverse mortgage. (I discuss this topic at length in Chapter 12.) Move in with your adult children. Cut down on expenses by moving to a location with a lower cost of living. Sell off those possessions on your "I don't need anymore" list. Go back to work to generate income doing things you enjoy, like leveraging your life experience and acquired skills into an encore career or turning a hobby into things to sell.

It all boils down to the fact that you have to run your life like a business and budget accordingly. If you're on a fixed income, determine how much money you need to live, including paying rent, food, insurance, and healthcare costs, plus a few extra dollars to blow on movies, restaurants, or shopping. Remember also to budget an extra 10% to 15% as a slush fund for the unexpected. It will then become easier to plug in the proceeds you might get from a home sale, home equity loan, or reverse mortgage to see what difference this could make to your quality of life.

Last but not least, don't be afraid to say, "I need help." Americans are by and large very generous people. Many of us have spent a good portion of our adult lives helping family and friends, people from our places of worship and in the greater community, and others in need around the world. It can be hard when the shoe is on the other foot to accept any form of aid or charity from others, but we're all in this together. Giving to others, whether it's helpful advice, a hug, or cash, is one of life's most satisfying experiences. Don't be afraid to accept the help and generosity of others.

Receiving help in a loving, grateful spirit and passing it forward when we're in a position to do so also brings out the best in us.

Chapter 11

Social Security

When should I take Social Security?"

This is one of the most common and pressing questions I hear from those nearing 60 years of age. As most of us know, the longer we wait to claim our benefits, the higher our monthly stipends will be. Our benefits increase 7% with each year we delay between age 62 to 66; they increase 8% with each year from 67 to 70. Obviously, waiting until age 70 gives the biggest return, and it's probably the right strategy assuming decent general health and a favorable life expectancy estimate. The bottom line for those who wait is compelling: a married couple following a well-formulated plan can expect an increased lifetime payout of $100,000 or more compared with taking early benefits. That's real money that can make a huge difference.

"But doesn't it make sense to take it sooner because isn't the whole system going under?" is the next thing I typically hear. In a word, no. If the system is going to fail, we'll have some strong indication of this several years before it happens. If we can benefit from the advice on these pages and keep our ears and eyes open to the warning signs (and not just what we get from the fear-mongering media), we should come out fine.

Nonetheless, the substantial mass of material on all the various options and individually tailored circumstances can be confusing even to the trained eye. Making sense of all the "what ifs," such as whether a wife should claim first on her own account or from the husband's benefits, seems to require a knowledge of advanced algebra. Getting good advice from a financial planner, accountant, or lawyer with specialized expertise is a safer bet. Many times, the cost of such counsel is an investment that more than pays for itself. The best bet when looking for a financial advisor is to hire one who works on an hourly basis instead of taking a commission of your earnings. Also pay attention to appearances, especially if a prospective advisor flamboyantly flaunts the trappings of his or her wealth, such as an overly luxurious office or bright red Ferrari, in a way that makes you feel uncomfortable. You want someone handling your money who exudes vigilance and care.

Since many of the policies and regulations regarding Social Security change over time, you should always double check anything in this book or that you hear about or read elsewhere to make sure you're not making decisions based on yesterday's news. The greatest sea change in recent years is granting gay married couples the same Social Security benefits as heterosexual couples. A careful reading of the Social Security website or updates from respected watchdogs and financial news commentators, along with advice from a trusted personal financial planning advisor, will keep you up to date.

As I mentioned earlier, the Social Security website is a refreshingly user-friendly and helpful site compared to most governmental online sources. In addition to a couple of really good retirement and life expectancy calculators, there are also helpful video tutorials and all the latest up-to-date material. Bottom line: the ability to apply online beats standing in line.

What I believe will not change anytime soon is my overarching recommendation to do everything you can to avoid taking your Social Security benefit starting at age 62. If the sky is falling and the demise of the whole system seems irrefutable (again, highly unlikely), then by all means go for it.

Also, to repeat, disregard this advice if you have good reason to believe you may not live well past full retirement age (this is age 66 for those born between 1943–1954, edging up in month increments until finally reaching age 67 for those born after 1967). And, obviously, you should take the money earlier if your financial situation is vulnerable and getting the check in the mail in a reduced amount will make a critical difference toward helping you meet your immediate needs.

Chapter 12

Reverse Mortgages A Good Reason to Always Be on Your Toes

It was 11:15 p.m. I was tucked in bed, trying to fall sleep with the TV on, when suddenly I felt the urge to reach for the phone and call the toll free number on the screen.

What sparked my interest was the opportunity to get the free, glossy "Seven Secrets of Reverse Mortgages" brochure being offered. I could see the wisdom of running a commercial like that at such a late hour because a lot of people stressed by money worries are still up then.

A very skillful salesman answered the phone and began asking me all sorts of questions. First, he wanted

"How much commission are you getting paid on this?"

to know my age. Sixty-two is the youngest I could be to qualify, and I told him I was 68 (not true). He then asked about my marital status and whether my spouse was younger or older.

I could tell he was reading from a script and that he was ready to drop me like a hot brick if I answered in any way that might disqualify me. I gave him a street address that he quickly looked up and confirmed was a condo. I sensed he was ready to pull the plug on me right then and there when he said, "We don't do reverse mortgages on condos."

"Oh, sorry, that's just my mailing address," I told him. "The home I own is in Maryland. Here's the right address."

Once I'd successfully navigated past the inquisition, the smoke and mirrors of salesmanship began. My under-the-covers investigation that night would prove to be both enlightening and disturbing. As I would soon learn, the salesperson's conduct with me was pretty much standard operating procedure for the industry.

The quagmire that an ill-advised reverse mortgage can become is ample justification alone for writing this book because it is such a fine example of how a good idea can easily go wrong. For that reason, it merits going into a fair amount of detail. Under the right conditions and with proper planning, taking a reverse mortgage can prove to be a wise choice to alleviate the financial stress so many seniors are experiencing these days, but many enter into this arrangement without taking responsibility for knowing all the facts and thus set themselves up for unfortunate consequences. To be frank, the reverse mortgage industry has earned a less than savory reputation due to some very bad practices.

One option to consider before going the reverse mortgage route is to look at taking out a home equity loan. If you qualify, a home equity loan has many of the same benefits as a reverse mortgage but with far fewer strings attached. The biggest advantage to consider is that the lender on a home equity loan can never foreclose on your home if you default. By contrast, reverse mortgages have much sharper teeth—you can be out on the street if you don't keep your end of the bargain. Before you take out a reverse mortgage, do some research to see if you qualify for some of the state and federally-sponsored home equity programs in your area, as they may work out better for you.

Most American seniors who own their homes tend to have the largest chunk of their life savings invested there, having built equity averaging about $110,000. For those who want to free up some of that money to help meet their expenses and who want to stay in their homes for the rest of their lives, either a reverse mortgage or a home equity loan can be the answer.

Too often, however, the decision to go into a reverse mortgage is made by people who are desperate and see it as a last resort. Attracted by the kind of advertisements like the one I saw on TV, they jump right into it. The problem is, knee-jerk decisions almost never work out well. Even the name "reverse mortgage" is misleading; a reverse mortgage is really a loan using the equity of your home as collateral, a loan that the lender calls in much like a foreclosure upon your death.

Reverse mortgages had been around for decades but didn't become big business until the real estate market and the U.S. economy plummeted in 2008. That's when many problems began. The major selling point of a reverse mortgage is the ability to stay in your home, guaranteed, for the rest of your life—as long as you read all the fine print and understand and comply with all the obligations. The major stipulations include residing in the house as your principal residence, paying all the taxes and home-owner's insurance on time, and keeping the house in good repair.

This is a serious risk for the 70% of seniors who elect to take their payment in one lump sum. Those who spend it without sufficient resources left to take care of their on-going bills and premiums five years down the line are left in the danger zone. Mercifully, this practice is now becoming a thing of the past, thanks to a new government regulation requiring lenders to hold back in escrow a portion of the proceeds (based again on life expectancy) to pay those bills directly.

Like every other major decision I discuss in this book, it's critical to educate yourself in order to plan carefully. Before you decide to take any action, it's crucial to know the right questions to ask that friendly salesperson offering the product. Again, the big prerequisite for planning, which also applies to almost every other option in this book, is coming to terms with your projected mortality. Armed with a good sense of your probable life expectancy, whether it's five years or 25, your options and choices become a lot clearer. Even if you aren't doing your own mortality estimate, the reverse mortgage lender is certainly running the same data and calculations on you to determine approximately how long they're likely to carry the loan.

The other major question you need to resolve before considering a reverse mortgage is obvious: do you really still need or want to live in your house? For many, this is a heavily emotional issue. Ask yourself if the attachment to the big house long after the children have left is due to a stubborn reluctance to accept change along the lines of "This is where our children were raised" or "We've celebrated the last 40 Christmases around this table."

The truth may be that the children have moved on with their lives. Is the fact that they come home once or twice a year worth being a slave to an expensive property that you can no longer afford? Here again, having a clear mind and weighing whether a reverse mortgage is the right choice for you means accepting the fact that you're getting older, your mortality is closer, and your children are gone. Keeping the money pit of your home when you're stretched beyond your means in the hopes of recapturing some of the good old days is a fool's game.

If you've done all the footwork required and still want to move forward on a reverse mortgage, here is what you need to know when dealing with my friend on the phone or any of his many colleagues. First of all, remember there is no law that keeps the salesperson you are talking to honest and forthright. Like other financial institutions and insurance companies, this company may have marble pillars holding up its roof, catchy marketing slogans, and bold logos designed to project a sense of security, caring, and stability, but far too often, the salespeople's chief motivation is getting the highest possible commission on a sale rather than looking for the product that best matches your needs.

This is why you need to be on your toes. You may hear terms like "government-insured, -guaranteed, -secured and/or -protected" to the point that you start to believe—falsely—that you're working with a federal program. You will also be told that you're not talking directly to the lender but dealing with an independent third party consultant who is on your side to advise you, like my friend who wanted to give me the seven secrets.

That last claim is partially true. In exchange for federally guaranteed loan insurance, all reverse mortgage lenders have agreed to work through this outside, unbiased consulting mechanism. But a funny thing happened in the financial downturn—the government cut the funding for this service. Nowadays, the only way for the counselor to get paid by the lender is to close the deal, creating a real conflict of interest. Thus, one of the first questions you should ask is, "How much commission are you being paid on this?" Consultants are not legally required to answer, but if they refuse to do so or give a highly unsatisfactory response, run quickly from this transaction.

Asking this kind of question may feel uncomfortably confrontational, but remember that this is business, and your health, well-being, and quality of life are at stake. Remember too that consultants want to give only the good news and are eager to avoid any discussion that might lead you to have second thoughts. They will try to bury any disclaimers about the possibility of you losing your home in the fine print or in the speed talk at the end of their commercials.

There are other quirks of human nature and our fragile egos at work that give the salesmen another advantage. No one wants to look like they don't know something when they're face to face with a slick agent holding a glossy brochure. Too often, the fear of looking stupid when confronted with terms and concepts you don't understand becomes a self-fulfilling prophecy. When you're in that desperation mode, you're especially prone to just glancing over the details and consenting with a nod of your dollar-sign-filled head because you've mentally already done the deal and cashed the check.

One such horror story appeared in the *New York Times* a few years ago chronicling how a woman was thrown out of her foreclosed home when her husband died. The couple's deal had been tied to the better interest rate based on the husband's older age. Had she been aware of this technicality and had she exercised her option to change to a slightly higher rate based on her age, she would never have lost the house she and her husband had shared for so many years.

Others have suffered similar fates simply because their deceased spouse's name was the only one listed on the deed. Happily, the outcry when this article was published forced regulators into action, but this situation makes it easy to understand why I had to be on my toes with my salesman.

"Say, I hear the government is getting ready to change things, and I won't be able to borrow as much money," I said.

"Yes, that's why you need to accelerate this quickly," the salesman replied, neglecting to tell me why this upcoming change was necessary and how it could protect me from abuse. Instead, he countered, "You'd better do this in the next 90 days or you won't get as much."

My salesman was doing all he could to foster a false sense of urgency, wanting me to send in my information, including a copy of my deed, as quickly as possible before this particular loophole closed.

That technique, by the way, is number six on the list of the biggest misleading claims by reverse mortgage companies as cited in a recent congressional report. Here's the full list of misinformation to watch out for:

1. The borrower will never owe more than the value of his or her home
2. Reverse mortgages are a government benefit and not a loan
3. A reverse mortgage is a lifetime loan, and therefore a borrower can never lose a loan

4. Borrowers can never lose their homes
5. Implied government affiliation
6. Implied time limit and limited geographical availability of reverse mortgages

But wait, there's more. The devil is in the pesky, complicated details that most of us skate past. A good example is the confusing little matter of how loan terms and interest rates can suddenly be reset due to falling equity. Research has demonstrated how easily consumers are confused by the whole notion of compounding interest on their reverse mortgages. They frequently are so focused on the short-term costs that they ignore the longer-term consequences, which can lead to unpleasant surprises later on. The consumer who elects to take a line of credit as payment for the reverse mortgage in lieu of getting a lump sum is especially vulnerable, as that stockpile of available funds can suddenly shrink without warning if the market value of the home falls.

This "confusion" brings up another uncomfortable topic that I need to be honest about—the fact that the decision-making abilities of many older Americans may be compromised due to cognitive difficulties resulting from the onset of Alzheimer's disease, dementia, or a wide range of other illnesses. Due to the potential for abuse, it might also be a good idea to protect seniors further by requiring a sound-mind statement from their physician before they can commit to any major financial transaction.

Other stories of unscrupulous sales techniques include cross-selling investments or insurance products, including convincing seniors to use their lump sum payment to purchase the deferred annuities some companies offer. It's a major red flag if the reverse mortgage lender tries to sell you on a new product. Again, run quickly away.

Also be aware that receiving the lump sum payment can affect your eligibility for Social Security and Medicare. The bureaucracy around stopping and starting these needs-based entitlements can be daunting. This can be avoided by placing assets in a trust or designating the distribution of funds to a trusted family member or loved one.

In conclusion, keep your eyes and ears open, ask questions, and remember to shop around. There are lots of players in the game, including many of the big name banks we all know so well, so do the research. Interest rates and closing costs can be very competitive. And remember that living well and exceeding a lender's calculation of your life expectancy is not only the best revenge but it can also make the whole idea of the reverse mortgage very profitable. Don't feel sorry for lenders, though. Federal insurance means they can't lose on the deal.

By the way, my telemarketing friend has yet to give up on me. He still calls from time to time to check in and is sure to ask whether I've given any further consideration to moving forward with my reverse mortgage. Surprisingly, the last e-mail I received from him was quite informative and more forthcoming about consumer protection. It was encouraging. Who knows, maybe reverse mortgage lenders are starting to clean up their acts.

Chapter 13

Long-Term Care Choices
at Home or at "the Home"

I t seems that every day when I open my mailbox, I find some piece of junk mail reminding me that I'm not getting any younger. The onslaught began once I reached age 50. It started with that thick AARP package complete with the personalized and embossed plastic membership card. Upon its arrival, many individuals who refuse to admit they're getting older bark, "I'm not there yet!" and unceremoniously dump the whole thing in the trash.

Truth be known, I'm happy to admit I'm a satisfied, card-carrying member of AARP. As the saying goes,

"Membership has its benefits," and the discounts I've received make it a great deal on everything from hotel stays to theater tickets. I didn't want to turn 50, but once I did, my outlook changed. Not only do I sometimes begin sentences to make a point with more emphasis and authority as a savvy senior, "Look, I'm 50 years old…" but I also realize that getting older means access to free or nicely discounted stuff. I might take some of what AARP talks about with a grain of salt, but going to their website is the equivalent of a sporting event in which I'm competing to see how much money I can save. Thus, it wasn't a surrender but a victory to turn 50 and sign up.

My mailbox is also clogged with flyers from local services providing everything from cleaning, errand running, and property management to round-the-clock nursing. I also receive glossy brochures about nearby retirement communities and assisted living facilities. Last but not least are the urgent pleas for me to consider buying long-term care insurance before it's too late. Thankfully, the junk mail stops short of mortuaries and cemeteries, which seem to relegate their outreach to formal-looking ads in the weekly penny saver.

Where they're wasting postage on me is in the realm of long-term care insurance. I bought mine in my early forties at a time when I was certainly not out shopping for it. Instead, it was something I was advised to do as part of my financial planning package. I pay $1,000 a year for this coverage. It was the right move for me, and I sleep better for having it, but to give a global statement that everyone needs it would be false.

One little unpleasant surprise I recently received was a notice out of the blue of a 28% premium increase. I called my insurance agent and asked why I'd received such a big increase. He told me that the insurance company underestimated the costs due to the fact that people are now living longer. The lesson: premiums aren't locked in. Understand that it's a gamble, and make sure it's a risk worth taking.

It's probably a sure bet that the bulk of these policies are sold to younger consumers when they're scared straight and experiencing firsthand the stark reality facing their ailing parents or other family members and friends.

In my opinion, the decision to buy this coverage is really easy if you don't have a large, close-knit family you can count on to take care of you when the time comes. The need for this is particularly acute in America and other industrialized Western countries where it's rare to find multi-generational households with family members taking care of each other through all phases of life. The idea of sending Grandma to a nursing home may be considered an egregious disgrace in many cultures, but not so here.

The trouble is, you have to make the decision to purchase long-term care before you actually need it. Here, too, you have to square yourself with the fact that we're all going to age and deteriorate and need some degree of care when we get older. Because Medicare is only going to cover the bare essentials to keep you alive, good coverage can make a night-and-day difference in the quality of the care you eventually receive.

A simple exercise to determine if long-term care coverage is the right move for you involves considering three questions:

1. Do you have a strong family unit or any form of support network that can take care of you?
2. Do you have enough money saved up to pay for such care out of pocket if the need arises?
3. Would you rather live independently for as long as possible?

If the answer to the first two questions is "No" and the question to question three is "Yes," then a long-term care policy makes perfect sense, but before you move forward on buying a policy, consider a few things.

First and foremost, make sure the provider will still be there five, 10, or 15 years later, when you need them. Double check to be sure the carrier is reputable, with a proven track record of longevity and strong financial standing.

Be aware and prepared for "the elimination period." That's the waiting period between the time you're disabled and when the policy starts paying. This period can last 30, 90, or even 120 days, and the longer you push it out, the cheaper the premium will be.

Understand the qualification requirements, coverage amounts, and limits. Don't be swayed by all the bells and whistles in the slick presentation but go right to the key details. What are the caps, and how much and how long will the policy continue to pay? There are options for home care, facility care, homemaker services, and so on. Ideally, the payment of benefits should move directly from the insurance carrier to the service provider because too often, if we get our hands on that money, we'll use it for something other than paying the bill it was designed for.

One other smart thing to do when buying this kind of coverage is to shop around. Car insurance has moved to a competitive marketplace where a company like esurance. com lists all the quotes and makes it easy to find the best deal to meet your needs. Don't be surprised to see a similar service pop up offering competitive long-term care insurance rates. Also, it may feel more practical to have a single company handle all your insurance needs, but that may not be the best deal. I am especially allergic to the word "bundle" (the way phone companies want to also sell you internet and cable on the same bill) that usually comes up when an insurance agent is in selling mode. By bundling, you're sacrificing what may be valuable options in the future for short-term convenience. If you drop one of the other services, your bundled long-term care policy may go down the drain with it. Resisting the urge to bundle also means you won't be locked in if a better service comes along later.

Also be aware that insurance companies make money hand over fist whenever people cancel their policies. It is common for consumers to lock themselves into expensive premiums only to get rid of their policies a few years later. Because we may be feeling well and are tired of making payments or because we want or need to spend our money elsewhere, we may be foolishly tempted to forget all about the certainty that we are going to one day need this care (unless we have opted for the route of living in a full service retirement community).

The other difficult and often troubling decision most of us must eventually face involves "going to the home." We all have a preconceived notion in our minds of what the "home" is like, and seldom is it a warm and fuzzy one. Fans of the *Golden Girls* sitcom might remember how Estelle Getty's character Sophie was always under threat of being sent to Shady Pines. (The *Golden Girls* were also quite progressive in one other area I mentioned earlier and will discuss more later, co-housing.)

As our country's demographics reflect an increasingly older population, the whole notion of retirement communities and goods and services for seniors is a promising growth area in the economy. The good news is that there are many options available today beyond the dreaded Shady Pines.

When my sister and I observed a brand new retirement community spring up not too far away from my parent's house, I was really quite surprised at how nice it was. Had I known about it earlier, I probably wouldn't have built a home for my parents. I would have had no problem buying a place there instead because of the wonderful sense of community, the helpful staff, and the nonstop social activities. The set-up is also transitional, meaning that residents move to different sections of the community as their needs change (from high functioning independence to hospice). Places like this are really trying to change the whole stigma around "going to the home."

Shady Pines or not, you're not going to know if a particular "home" is the right place for you unless you actually go see it. Of course, the person selling you on the place is "following the script" and is going to present an idealized, deodorized picture. The brochure might show a warm, cozy, and elegant public face replete with chandeliers, but the real test is to see what the faraway rooms are like. What the person might have presented may be true but also may omit some of the less attractive and uncomfortable parts of the equation. Where it can get dicey is in determining what the quality of life is like for those who start losing their independence.

If you really want to know the nitty-gritty truth before making a decision about a retirement community, here is one stealth strategy to consider: why not go undercover? Treat it like a game, a research project, just to see what a prospective place is like. Find one or two possibilities in the area and pay a visit. Imagine what it would be like if this were your final move to the place where you were eventually going to die. Ask yourself two critical questions. First, if something happens, do you want to be in a situation where no one will find you until it's too late and the police will have to break down the door only to discover your poor starving cat has begun feasting on your

Don't let this happen to you!

face? Second, if something happens, do you want to be in a place where you know you'll at least be taken care of?

"If I go there and they get their meat-hooks into me, I'm never going to get out," you might fear, as if iron gates will slam behind you once you cross the threshold. But that isn't the case. You're only exploring the alternatives that exist. It doesn't mean you're committing to them.

When you get to your prospective retirement community, talk to the staff and some of the residents. Take the full tour. To really get the inside scoop, ask if the facility needs volunteer help. You might be asked to help serve meals, assist with recreational activities, or drive people around. You will have many opportunities to talk to the residents as well as the people who work there. Gauge their experiences. After a short while, you will have a solid knowledge base from which to make the right decision.

Volunteering at a retirement community is probably one of those ideas that makes sense but at the end of the day isn't something a lot of us are going to do. Again, while we're relatively healthy and independent, it's easy to push the whole idea out of our minds and bury it beneath a stack of other deferred decisions.

As for me, not only do I sleep better because I have long-term health insurance but I also have peace of mind that nobody is going to send me to Shady Oaks. This is because I'm not going to leave such an important decision to others, to my flawed assumptions, or to wishful thinking.

Whether you are considering long-term care insurance policies, retirement communities, or any of the other choices I discuss in this book, information is power. It allows us to be buyers in the best sense of the word, making choices based on what we know and what is important to us as opposed to being "sold" by someone who is trying to convince us of something.

Chapter 14

Life Insurance and Life Settlements

We've all had a friend or colleague lose a family member. We've all picked up the newspaper and read about some tragedy random enough that it could have happened to anyone. In more cases than not, that's what's behind the decision to go out and purchase life insurance.

"Buy insurance" is yet another cautionary tale that should remind us that when our emotions are in play, we don't always make sound decisions. When we don't take the time to do our homework, we often don't know enough to ask the agent many of the basic questions we should ask to best inform our decision. Instead, we cede our power and put ourselves in the often dubious hands of the sales agent.

It is my business to know how insurance companies work, how agents are trained, and what they think. What I see behind the scenes is not always pretty. Those in the industry will tell you off the record that their sales techniques aren't necessarily designed to guide their clients toward what they actually need. Instead, they're designed to steer clients toward the most expensive products in order to generate the best possible commissions. Again, that's why asking that simple, albeit annoying, question—"How much commission are you getting paid for these different kinds of policies?"—can help level the playing field.

Agents want to steer you to purchase whole life policies, and they present them with all sorts of great-looking graphs and charts. They want you to think, "Oh, yes, I think I can handle that premium," when in truth your needs would probably be better served with a much cheaper term policy. The fact is, most life insurance should not be purchased as an investment but instead to cover contingencies. If you plan to keep a whole life policy for 15 to 30 years as a form of tax-free savings, it may make sense, but before you commit, beware of all the layers of fees you will be charged, fees that can eat into your investment. On this point alone, you may need to shop around to make sure you're getting the best terms.

Keep in mind that the insurance business is a highly profitable one, with 85% of all policies lapsing without ever going into effect. People often come to view their life insurance as a burden and a liability, so when things get tight, that quarterly premium is often the first expense to be cut. That's music to the insurance company's ears. You never hear about them having to lay off employees during a recession, nor do you ever see foreclosure signs on their stately office buildings. In fact, so few death benefits are paid these days that industry lobbyists are petitioning lawmakers to lower the threshold amount they have to hold in reserve for that purpose.

Even the non-profit AARP is in on the big money, quietly receiving several hundred million dollars each year from insurance companies for the policies they sell to their huge membership. While there are clear savings when buying as a member of a large group, there are also looming questions about how ethical it is for a group that promotes itself as protecting senior citizens' rights to be in bed with an industry that does so little to safeguard consumers. I think it's smart to question how this potential conflict of interest could affect you before making such a purchase.

There is also another little secret insurance companies don't want you to know: if you buy a term life insurance policy that is nearing the end of its time limit, you have the right to convert it to a whole life plan *without having to take a new medical exam*. Even if you have a life-threatening condition, you cannot be turned away. The insurance companies don't want you to know this because it means they lose the bet, and they don't like to be outsmarted.

Life settlements are another way to win the bet against the insurance companies. This strategy turns your life insurance policy into a cash generator that can make your older years more comfortable. If you ask older people what a life settlement is, most will not know the answer, but those who acquaint themselves with this concept find it a very pleasant surprise to discover that their life insurance policy is not an outgoing liability but rather a valuable asset that they don't have to die to use. Thanks to a U.S. Supreme Court ruling in the early 1900s, your life insurance policy is private property that can be legally sold. It has cash value no different than a car, a house, or a painting. Life settlements are not for everyone, especially if the specific needs for which you originally purchased the policy are still in effect, but for those who either no longer want or need the policy or who can no longer afford the premiums, a life settlement can be an attractive option.

People over age 65 who go this route can receive a one-lump-sum cash payment for their policy from the life settlement company that in most cases will exceed the cash surrender value by eight to 10 times. There are also now hybrid life settlements that allow the person to get the best of both worlds—to retain a portion of the death benefit but also receive the cash payouts.

Life settlement companies take over the on-going payment of premiums, and in return, recipients release to the company all their financial and medical records and check in with a company social worker or nurse every three months to update their health status. The general rule of thumb regarding how policies are appraised is this: the lower the premium and the shorter the life expectancy, the higher the payment.

Often seniors will think at the end of their term policies, "I'm not as healthy as I was when I got the term. I'll never be able to afford a new policy." For them, exercising the secret option to convert their nearly worthless expiring term life policy into a whole life policy without an additional medical exam can be a windfall.

In many cases, the decision to pursue a life settlement should be thoroughly discussed with your family. In fact, when a family gets together around a life settlement discussion, it is almost never regretted. There are many remarkable stories of how the proceeds from life settlements helped clients not only make their later years more comfortable but also gave them a chance to fulfill lifelong dreams such as arranging a multi-generational vacation to bring the whole family together, maybe for the last time.

Others have used the proceeds in some very creative ways. One person sold a policy because he didn't want his children fighting over their inheritance. The family had owned a farm for generations, so he decided to use the extra capital to restock cattle as a strategy to keep the family intact. Everyone would have to pool together to work the farm instead of quarreling over the money and then quickly blowing through it.

Life settlements can also be done privately. Some who can no longer afford their premiums may be able to structure a private life settlement within their family. Admittedly, it might be very challenging to sit down with family members and admit that you can't pay the premiums. It also brings up that death discussion that nobody likes to have. But the payoff, again, is the surprising amount of weight that is lifted off your shoulders when you get other people involved. In exchange for being a beneficiary, a family member or family members pooled together can serve the same function as a life settlement company, agreeing to make a cash payment and to take over the premiums.

Life settlements have better consumer protection and governmental oversight of transactions than most of the other services I discuss. I know this for a fact because I worked with the government regulators to help craft most of these regulations in the early 1990s. But similar to warnings for other services, consumers need to exercise caution when agents try to cross-sell other services or fail to adequately educate the consumer on their obligations. (Bear in mind that it's not like getting cash from an ATM; there is an ongoing relationship between the consumer and the settlement provider.) Do research on the company, look at longevity and reputation, and know that taking the money in a lump sum payout is a good hedge against being victimized in the event the company goes under.

A good life settlement company will work with you to make the arrangement serve your needs. Instead of

Chapter 15

Wills and Other Legal Safeguards You Can't Afford to Ignore

W hen I'm on airplanes, I talk to people all the time. The usual introductory questions "What do you do?" and "What are you working on?" invariably open up bigger discussions.

In one of these onboard sessions, a woman about my age or possibly a little older asked me whether she really needed to make a will. After we chatted for a while, she concluded, "Well, I'm just going to let my husband make all those decisions."

"Do you really want to leave that burden on him?" I countered.

"I don't have anything to leave."

"You must have something of value," I protested.

"Yeah, but I don't have anything that's really going to amount to anything."

I quickly looked her over and noticed her hand. "What about your wedding ring?"

"I'll probably want that to go to my son and whoever he marries, but I don't know if I'll like her," she chuckled.

"That's something you should write down."

Wills are something people are horribly resistant to creating, but they are nowhere nearly as complicated as most individuals think. Even a handwritten letter that is signed and witnessed qualifies as a will. You can even find fill-in-the-blank forms online or at the library.

Do-it-yourself kits are also available at office supply stores like Staples or Office Depot. Making a will should be something every responsible adult does. You're not an exception unless you don't care about the people in your life and the decisions they will be faced with when you become incapacitated and die. Your wishes need to be heard, but this means you need to make them formally known first. Not doing so tears families apart and leaves them fighting over what each thinks is best.

Not having a will (and an updated one at that) may also make it a good deal for the IRS and a bad one for your loved ones. A magazine article I recently read about estate planning failures of the rich shocked me because I assumed that wealthy and famous people would have their acts together. After all, they can afford the best advisors.

The actor James Gandofini, for example, died suddenly of a heart attack, and 80% of his 70-million-dollar estate was exposed to taxes because he didn't have a financial plan in place. If Phillip Seymour Hoffman had acknowledged his mortality and consulted an estate planner, his 35-million-dollar estate would have had a lesser tax bill than $12 million. Paul Walker had $25 million but probably thought he would have a lot of time in the future to deal with the details. Ed Koch and Robin Gibbs were other sorry examples of people who didn't take the time to deal with their estates.

In many states, if you don't have a plan, your estate goes into probate, and then you've got strangers making decisions about what to do with your assets. All that could be prevented by getting a will and writing down how you wish your assets to be distributed. It's simple to do and can relieve a big burden. By checking this off your list now, you can avoid being hit with a panic attack when everything begins to go wrong and you find yourself scrambling to resolve your assets when you're not in a good position to think anything, much less everything, through.

While I'm at it, you should also write up a living will and a durable power of attorney for healthcare matters. The living will stipulates your preferences for end-of-life care and treatment. The durable power of attorney appoints someone you trust to carry out your wishes if you cannot advocate for yourself. Again, ask yourself: do you want to be the hostage of a healthcare institution that's forcing tubes down your throat to jack up the bill? Just as bad, do you want to put a bigger strain on public assistance against your unexpressed wishes? Taking fifteen minutes to write down your wishes in a living will and durable power of attorney can prevent all that. These documents are designed to give people the right to make decisions for you—decisions that you approve of—when you no longer can.

Trusts are another tool to consider. They have the reputation of only being for the wealthy, but it can make a lot of sense to set one up if you have assets over $100,000, which may be in the equity you have in your home.

Trusts are like having your valuables in an armored strong box impenetrable to attack. Creditors cannot get to them, nor can an ex-wife or somebody who's suing you. Trusts can also be beneficial for saving estate taxes. Proceeds from life settlements or reverse mortgages can also be put in the trust to minimize putting your needs-based entitlements eligibility at risk (think Social Security, Medicare, and Medicaid).

There are many different options to choose from. If you can afford it, I recommend spending time with a fee-based financial planner to find out what's best for you. If you can't afford it, you can often get someone at your bank or at a big, well-known entity like JP Morgan or UBS to give you free advice. Remember that asking for help isn't always charity, so let go of your ego and insecurities. Play the age card! Say something like, "Can you explain this for me? I'm old and I need a trust." A lot of people enjoy helping and like the good karma of providing assistance to others. Either way, you get the help you need, help that you truly can't afford to do without.

Chapter 16

Trial by Fire

Once we break through the barriers and are willing to start talking about the all-too-taboo subject of mortality, we begin to notice a shift inside ourselves. With this breakthrough, we begin to summon the courage to confront the truth and start taking some positive first steps to attain true peace of mind rather than behaving as though we're oblivious to that elephant in the middle of the room that's hiding under the tablecloth.

Putting the strategies I have talked about into action may feel uncomfortable and even painful at first, but think of it instead as exposing and dressing a wound in order for it to heal. This is a far better choice than leaving it untreated to fester and worsen.

Trust me, the process of writing this book has helped me reevaluate a lot of my own attitudes and actions. Just because my name is on the cover doesn't give me a free pass. As I often say, I am truly a work in progress. This isn't some catch-all, clichéd excuse but rather helps me accept how my life is in constant flux. As my circumstances change, I need to constantly check in to update and revise.

Something that often changes as people age is how they view end-of-life care. For example, in the past, perhaps you wrote down that you wanted all heroic measures taken to revive you in an emergency but later you realized that you can't imagine being kept alive in a vegetative state hooked up to machines. Because your ideas, understanding, and knowledge evolve, you need to frequently revisit and update your thinking. That's why the estate planning I did over 10 years ago has needed some occasional tweaking.

Benjamin Franklin nailed it when he said that nothing is certain in life except death and taxes. Everything else is a benefit. Our task is to make the most out of life that we can. Our bodies, our states of health, and our relationships all change. People come and go. Our experiences and life lessons alter us and open our minds to new attitudes.

Even though my job involves sitting at a desk and looking at life expectancies for other people, it's still a slap in the face when it strikes close to home. I can prepare myself and run through the drills and hypothetical scenarios, attempting to imagine what the outcome might be, but the reality of it is quite different as it unfolds.

Again, this underscores why it's so important to do as much preplanning as possible so we're not hit with everything all at once when we're at our most vulnerable.

One illusion I had to confront while writing this book involved what I would do if I became sick and needed help from people dear to me—what I call my care-giving team. Taking off my rose-colored glasses, I finally accepted that almost all the people I care about and would want to be around in my old age are older than I am and in much worse health. If things progress as they naturally should, these individuals will be gone before I need them.

Giving up this fantasy of receiving help from my care-giving team was depressing and made it difficult to fall back to sleep in the middle of the night, but once my initial emotion subsided and I dealt with my fears and anxieties, it actually turned out to be quite an enlightening experience.

Handling the passing of my brother Tracy and helping my aging parents with their financial predicaments at the time of this writing often felt like I was conducting a real-time test of many of the approaches outlined in the book. I am grateful to report that the end results brought some astonishing if not miraculous payoffs.

My experience in taking a dose of my own medicine brings to mind a classic story about Mahatma Gandhi. People would travel from all over India, often on foot over long distances, to have an audience with him. One woman made the arduous journey with her son and waited in a long line until finally her time came. Then she said, "Mahatma-

Ji, please tell my son to stop eating sugar." Gandhi's only reply was to ask her to come back in one week.

The woman did as she was told and returned for a second audience. The message the second time was equally terse. Gandhi turned to her young son and said, "Stop eating sugar." The woman was understandably upset that she'd had to make a second difficult trip to hear this. "Why couldn't you have told him this the first time?" she exclaimed.

Gandhi turned to her and replied, "Madame, last week I ate sugar. So now at least I can say from a battle-tested point of view that I am not asking any of us to do anything that I haven't been willing to go through myself!"

Within my own family, the pre-planning and preparations I did leading up to my brother's death brought with them a number of blessings in addition to the celebratory wake I described earlier. Given what we'd been dealing with for years, I didn't have any expectations that my parents' deep-seated behavioral patterns would ever change. They were stuck in a holding pattern of confusion, fear, and despair around the fact that my brother was dying. It was if they'd put the rest of their lives on hold and had no time or interest in the rest of their family and friends and the activities they'd once loved to do.

During the final years of his life, my brother often played the guilt card. Among other issues, I think he blamed my father for not buying him an expensive helmet when he played high school football that could have prevented his concussions. Feeling deprived became his rationale for acting as he did. Whenever the phone rang, my parents jumped to answer it. They had to do everything they could to help Tracy because, after all, he was dying.

"We're all dying," I told my parents repeatedly. I tried to bring the point home by telling them that the threat of danger and imminent death wasn't just the reality for Tracy but for their other two children as well. I concluded, "You don't need to talk to me every time I get on an airplane or talk to Becky every time she gets in a car to drive to work. You don't need to say 'I love you' to one another every time you walk out the door to go to the store."

Seeing the snowballing effect on the people I loved as Tracy's health declined was torture. Whenever my phone rang, it was always drama, either my parents fighting or my brother creating havoc with his substance abuse. Trust me, this gave me pause to think before calling home. Typically, my brother was drunk and my father was yelling at his dying son to stop drinking. Finally, even the hospice nurse said, "If he wants to drink, let him drink." Of course, confronting his substance abuse a few decades earlier might have changed the outcome, but it was too late now, something that remains a very bitter pill to swallow.

Even when she went out, my mother's cell phone seemed to ring every couple of minutes with nonstop drama. When I took her to see Cher in concert, I had to take her phone away from her. I lied and told her that I was trying to connect her to the network, but I was actually blocking her calls so she could enjoy the concert.

Going home for holidays was a mixed bag, a time for family togetherness but also for conflict. Tracy was often drunk. Drug dealers were always lurking. All that and more made it tough to be there.

A few months after Tracy's passing, I noticed that the conversations I was having with my parents were changing. I could sense palpable relief and even joy, though I'm not sure my parents will ever admit their lives are less stressful without their son. My mother once said to me, "You know, Scotty, I was there when he took his first breath, and I was there when he took his last, and a lot of mothers don't get to experience that. You go before your children." Under the circumstances, I am grateful my mother choose to view this a gift.

Today, ironically, I see my parents growing as a couple. They are starting to acknowledge how their own mortality is going to come into play, accepting what they need to do to start living each day like it's the rest of their lives.

Now, when I call my mother, we talk about things besides my brother. We talk more than we have in years, and it's joyous. My parents are now doing things that seniors are supposed to do, like chatting about where they're going to eat or taking a nap when they feel like it. They're getting their first real Christmas tree in years instead of that two-foot-tall plastic thing they used to put on top of the coffee table. My mother has even started to socialize and make new friends. She looks forward to her Friday nights at the karaoke bar, something she never permitted herself to do before Tracy died.

"I faced it all and I stood tall and did it my waaay!"

Maybe they have some guilt about getting their lives back, but I think it diminishes with each passing day, though they'll always wonder what might have been. One symbolic message came to me about a week after Tracy's funeral, when I decided to erase all the voicemails on my phone. For some unexplained reason, one message refused to be deleted—one in which my brother had called to thank me for giving him a cell phone. Inexplicably, he wasn't drunk but was very calm and lucid. It was the Tracy we all knew was inside him. I told my mother about it, and we cried. It was a healthy mourning discussion.

I know I played a valuable role in my parents' process of closure and my own by planning my brother's passing and doing the best I could for the loved ones around me. Their lives are more loving and less stressful as a result. This coupled with the financial planning we've engaged in has enabled them to enjoy themselves and take better care of each other, which is what my dream has always been for them.

If my parents can come through this trial by fire, any of us can. In the spirit of hope and faith, I encourage you to embrace these heartfelt words of advice and practical tools of the trade and begin the wonderful process of freeing yourself from worry while getting older and wiser in your own golden years.

Printed in the USA
CPSIA information can be obtained
at www.ICGtesting.com
JSHW082345140824
68134JS00020B/1891

9 781630 476236